AN
OLD-FASHIONED
CHRISTMAS

AN OLD-FASHIONED CHRISTMAS

IRIS GRENDER

HUTCHINSON OF LONDON

Hutchinson & Co. (Publishers) Ltd
3 Fitzroy Square London W1P 6JD

London Melbourne Sydney Auckland
Wellington Johannesburg and agencies
throughout the world

First published 1979

© Iris Grender 1979
Illustrations © Hutchinson Publishing Group 1979

Set in Gloucester Light

Printed in Great Britain by The Anchor Press Ltd
and bound by Wm Brendon & Son Ltd
both of Tiptree, Essex

ISBN 0 09 136040 4

DECK THE HALLS 9

EVERGREENS 11

IN THE WOODS 16

TREASURES FROM THE BEACH 17

THE CHRISTMAS TREE 18

**THE NATIONAL BIRD OF
THE BRITISH ISLES 24**

CHRISTMAS CARDS 27

PAPER DECORATIONS 30

CHRISTMAS CRACKERS 32

CAROLS AND CAROLLING 35

RULES FOR CAROLLERS 38

A LANTERN-BEARER 38

CAROLS 39

TOYS AND GIFTS TO MAKE 47

ST NICHOLAS 50

FILLING THE STOCKING 55

MAKING GIFTS 58

CANDLEMAKING 64

GIFT WRAPPING 66

THE FEAST 71

FOOD 72

DRINKS 83

THE FESTIVITIES 85

GAMES 86

TRICKS 89

TWELVE DAYS OF CHRISTMAS 92

CLEARING UP 95

LETTING IN CHRISTMAS.

INTRODUCTION

The lives of the ancient Druids revolved around the pastoral year. They celebrated the sun's rebirth after the winter solstice and began their festivities on the shortest day of the year, 12 December. The wild Norsemen of Northern Europe had a candlelit festival which was timed to brighten the darkest days in the natural calendar. The Romans indulged themselves in the cold winter with the orgies of Saturnalia. The early Christians incorporated all of these festivals and ceremonies into the church calendar.

Now we celebrate Christ's Mass every year on the twenty-fifth day of December. It's Christmas Day! It's also a little of ancient Druid superstition, a Norse candle glow and a taste of heady wine from Saturnalia. A good old-fashioned British Christmas is made up of all these.

At Christmas play and make good cheere,
For Christmas comes but once a yeere!

This couplet was first recorded by Thomas Tusser in the sixteenth century. A modern version of the traditional rhyme is:

Christmas comes but once a year
And when it comes it brings good cheer,
A pocketful of money, and a cellar full of beer,
And a good fat pig to last you all the year.

And yet another version of the same rhyme is:

Bounce, buckram, velvet's dear,
Christmas comes but once a year;
And when it comes, it brings good cheer,
But when it's gone it's never near.

Into this book have gone the simplest and most traditional ideas for toys, gifts, decorations, games, Christmas food and Christmas carols. For most of us the problem is one of 'Where to begin?' in our Christmas preparations. For this reason all of the most basic ideas concerning Christmas are included in this book, so that you and your children can discover the wonders of a truly traditional festive season.

THE NATIVITY

Little Jesus, sweetly sleep, do not stir,
We will lend a coat of fur.

And so a cluster of little children sing as they act out the Nativity play. This is where Christmas begins for most of us, with a visit to the school or church. The tradition of acting out biblical stories belongs to the early history of the church. Long ago only the clerics could read. To help the kings, nobles and peasants to understand the Bible stories, scenes were acted in the church. When the language became too casual and irreverent, the priests moved the site of the play to the churchyard. Once out of the reverent atmosphere of the church the actors could relax and the language became even worse, and so they moved to the village green.

When we go along to watch the Nativity play we know the reality of the children dressed up in striped tea-towels and old sheets. There may be one child representing the Star of Bethlehem with a gold star fixed to the brow. For the friends and relations of the children watching the play, every child is a star. As our children re-enact the Christmas story they are learning the meaning of Christmas and perhaps it is also a time when most of us count our blessings.

THE CRIB

In pre-Christian times the Romans gave each other clay dolls when they celebrated their religious festivals. Naturally the early Christians couldn't ban the customs of so many generations of Romans, and so the crib surrounded by clay figures representing shepherds, angels, wise men and animals has been handed down to us from the early Romans. The crib was used in church as a visual aid for telling the story of the nativity.

For making a crib use natural materials. Twigs and straw are useful for the stable and the manger. The little figures can be made from New Clay which doesn't need baking or from modelling wax. Older children may be able to carve figures for the crib from domestic candles, which have a delicate translucent appearance. (Wax figures must stand well away from radiators or they warp.)

Use the finest fabrics from the ragbag for dressing the figures or they look clumsy. Since the figures wear long clothes there is no need to model legs. Give them bell-shaped bases to help them stand firmly.

Begin with a firm cardboard box for making the stable. Twigs and straw can be glued on to that. Fir cone pieces can be used as tiles.

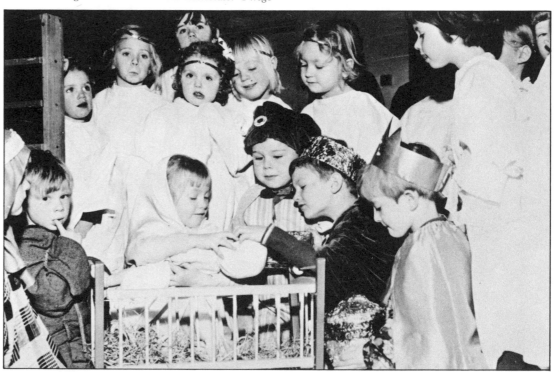

PART I

DECK THE HALLS

With holly and ivy,
So green and so gay,
We deck up our houses
As fresh as the day;

With bay and rosemary
And laurel complete;
And every one now
Is a king in conceit.

EVERGREENS

When evergreens are brought indoors at Christmas they are a Christian symbol of everlasting life. When the civilized world was young the pagans used evergreens as a similar sign. Evergreens for them were a symbol that all life was not dead.

In Victorian times, every flower or piece of foliage in a posy had a meaning. The evergreen promised that 'our friendship will be evergreen'. Consequently, evergreens became fashionable symbols on Christmas cards.

Compliments of the Season

CHRISTMAS WREATHS

A wreath on the door offers visitors a hospitable welcome. They are a recent innovation in the British Isles which came over to us from the United States along with Santa's reindeer and the song, 'Jingle Bells'. The custom of a wreath on the door was one introduced in America by Scandinavian immigrants.

Wreaths are simple to make. A firm wreath can be made by using two rings of cane; also, it is possible to obtain wire frames from some florists' shops. (Old wire coat hangers can be used although they tend to buckle.) Tie a small ring inside a large one at the top. Holly is the traditional evergreen for a wreath, but any form of evergreen can be used. Bind on 18-inch lengths of thick, close-leaved evergreen such as yew and box with florist's or gardening wire. Work on a flat surface and wind wire round and round to secure greens on base frame. Add holly, ivy and a red ribbon.

An attractive decoration can be a spray to hang on the letter box. Simply place long pieces of foliage at the back and short pieces at the front and fix together with gardening wire. Tie with a tinsel ribbon.

Evergreens stay fresh if they are plunged into a bucket of water as soon as they're picked. Leave them in the water for as long as possible before making arrangements.

THE HOLLY AND THE IVY

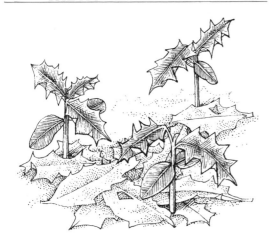

When Christ first set foot upon the ground a small plant sprang up where he stepped. It was the holly bush. The form of the holly leaves and the colour of the berries foretold the Crucifixion. The sharp spines of the leaves warned of the crown of thorns and the red berries symbolized the shedding of Christ's blood for mankind.

Holly was revered as a sacred tree long before the early Christians adopted it, and it is considered lucky. The custom of using holly as Christmas decorations is normally attributed to the Romans who handed around branches of evergreen holly during the celebration of Saturnalia. Many superstitions surround the holly. In some areas hedgers still believe it's unlucky to cut holly, and you might see a tall wild bush in the midst of a trimmed hedge.

Fires made with holly wood are remarkable. When every other piece of wood is soaked with winter rain the holly burns and crackles merrily. With its sharp spines of defence and its red berries of fire, holly cheered the winter gloom in the homes of ancient Britons.

Most evergreens are slow-growing and holly is one of the slowest. When holly is drastically pruned it responds by growing into a distorted shape. Gather holly sparingly. Leave plenty of berries for the birds. Bitter holly berries are one of the last items on the winter menu of the birds. In late winter the birds disperse the seeds and ensure the survival of the holly.

Seedling holly trees spring up everywhere beneath mature holly trees. A very traditional gift can be made by planting a holly seedling in a pot and surrounding it with variegated ivy. This needs to be done well before Christmas to allow the plants time to establish themselves.

Ivy flowers in the autumn and the berries appear in the spring. Long ago the purplish black berries were associated with the devil. Ivy was brought indoors to keep demons away from the house. Ivy is poisonous, but the wood was attributed with special properties. 'To cure an alcoholic or a child with whooping cough let them drink from a cup made of ivy wood.'

Strands of ivy look effective trailing from a basketful of mixed evergreens. An old candlestick with ivy fixed to the sides must be one of the most effective yet simplest Christmas decorations ever devised.

It is not difficult to find ivy, even in the city. The moment an area is left uncultivated ivy takes over, clambering up trees, fences and old buildings to reach the light. It is a tough plant, so always remember to take secateurs along to gather it. Look for it on building sites, railway embankments, in dark shady hedges and at the sides of football pitches. Pull strands from trees for the best trailing pieces. This will give the tree a chance to breathe.

MAGICAL MISTLETOE

Mistletoe was the sacred plant of the Druids. It was cut by the high priest of the cult with a golden sickle. Mistletoe grows as a parasite in gnarled cracks of old deciduous trees such as oak, elm or apple.

Our pagan forefathers believed that the mistletoe plant held the life of the parent tree during the winter. White mistletoe berries contained the precious seminal fluid of the tree. So mighty was the power of the mistletoe that it became known as 'Heal-all', which suggests that it was used as a herb to cure many common ailments. (Herbalists never sample a herb unless they know another herbalist who has sampled an old remedy and survived.)

The early Christians incorporated the fertility symbol of the Druids into their own teaching. Mistletoe became the evergreen symbol of ever-lasting love.

THE LEGEND OF BALDER THE SUN GOD AND THE ARROW OF MISTLETOE

The god of the sun, Balder, was mighty and beautiful. He was greatly loved by the other gods for his beauty, warmth and splendour. They cast spells for his protection. Neither fire, nor earth nor water could harm him.

Loki, the fierce god of evil, was jealous of Balder, the mighty and beautiful. He set out to destroy him. With evil delight he discovered that mistletoe had been forgotten when the gods cast their protective spells. Loki took a bough of mistletoe and sharpened it into a fine arrow. He placed the mistletoe arrow in

the hand of Hoder, the blind god. Using the hand of Hoder, Loki took aim, and the arrow went spinning straight to Balder, killing him.

The gods were grieved and angry. They brought Balder back to life and made the plant of mistletoe swear never to harm another mortal or immortal soul. Since that day a kiss beneath the mistletoe has been a year-long promise of protection from fire and earth and water.

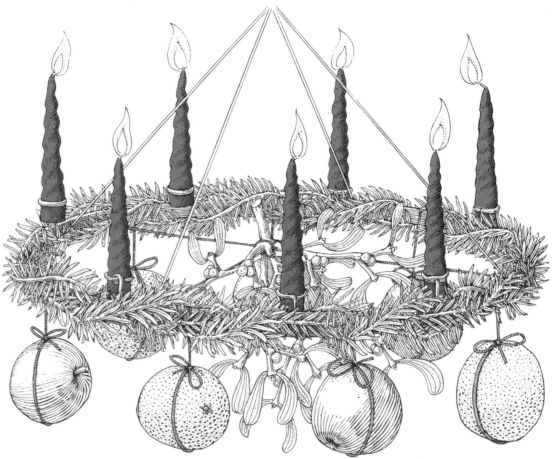

A KISSING RING

Make a kissing or Advent ring with a cane frame which can be saved from year to year. The frame of an old lampshade can serve as a satisfactory alternative. The shape of the frame should be round with two supports making an 'X' in the centre of the ring.

Cover the frame by tying on any kind of evergreen, though yew is usually used. Suspend four apples and three oranges or satsumas from the ring held horizontally like a crown. Crab apples make a good substitute for apples. They are lighter to suspend and were the bitter sharp apples the Britons used before apples became cultivated.

Make wire candle holders to stand upright from the ring by bending gardening wire to fit. Fix seven small candles into the holders. Mistletoe should be suspended from the centre; it's good luck to kiss and be kissed beneath the mistletoe.

YEW, THE TREE OF POWERFUL DEFENCE

The yew is the ancient Briton of trees. A yew can live for as long as a thousand years, so it isn't surprising that our ancestors revered it. The Northern Europeans decked their houses with evergreens, as the symbol of everlasting life and life to be reborn. Their celebration evergreens included yew despite the fact that yew is poisonous to man and cattle. Yew hedges can still be seen today planted around old churches or old houses. Yew was thought to be a defence against witches who raised storms upon buildings unless they were protected.

The best of the English longbows were made of yew, and the trees were carefully nurtured for this purpose. This added weight to the superstition that yew was a strong defence against evil.

COMFORTS

In spring, summer and autumn the nobility carried bunches of sweet-scented herbs which they held under their noses whenever they encountered evil smells. In wintertime when there were no sweet herbs they carried an orange spiked with cloves; the poor substituted crab apples for the oranges and these became known as 'Poor Man's Comforts'.

Apples and oranges spiked with cloves have now found their way into the bowl of punch. Another use for them is among the decorations where they scent the house sweetly. It would be best to make these decorations near Christmas as they do not

last for more than a few days. Tie a narrow red or green ribbon four ways around a satsuma or clementine. Spike it with a pattern of cloves. Push a ribbon through the centre of the top ribbons by which to suspend it. (Humble crab apples give out a spicy scent too if they're spiked in the same way.)

IN THE WOODS

In the autumn the ground is covered with useful materials. The best time to take a walk in the woods or in parkland is just after a high wind when the fruits from nut trees and fir trees will have fallen to the ground.

FIR CONES

Cone swag An attractive swag for the door can be made from fir cones of various sizes and types. To make an unusual 'flower', cut out the inner scales of a large cone and spread out the outer sections. Then glue a small cone in the centre. The swag can be decorated with bright coloured ribbons, small glass balls and greenery. Spray over with a coat of clear varnish when complete.

Clusters Paint fir cones gold or silver, leave them natural or add a little 'snow' made from shoe whitener or spray. Tie together with string. Hang the cones in clusters with red or green ribbons.

Cobwebs Dab the cones around the stems with glue. Wind on coloured thread to make cobwebs. Suspend the cones from the tree.

Fir cone tree Using a rubber solution glue, pile fir cones on to a paper plate in the shape of a tree with the largest cones at the base. Top the tree with a foil star to make a centrepiece for the table.

Glitter Coat the tips of the fir cones with glue and dip them into glitter. Mix some glue with white paint or shoe whitener and glitter to make a snowy effect.

BEECHNUTS AND ACORNS

Our ancient ancestors the Druids revered the oak as the father of the trees. Beechnuts and acorns were gathered as a subsistence diet when the harvest was poor. A few beechnuts and acorns among the decorations would lend an old-fashioned and traditional look to them. Use those with stalks or they will be difficult to suspend. Glue the acorns firmly into their cups, and paint them with gold or silver paint. Beechnuts can be simply wrapped in silver foil: take the nut out of its case and wrap it in the foil and then glue it back in its case. These small decorations may well be all that's needed to decorate a dainty tree.

TWIGS

Let children spread an armful of fallen twigs out on plenty of newspaper and paint them. If the weather is mild this can be done in the garden to save mess. Silver twigs can be used for making a bauble tree or for mixing in with dried flowers. Put the twigs in a pot filled with earth and hang sweets from them.

TREASURES FROM THE BEACH

A fossil, a piece of sea-washed glass, a dried starfish, or a dried seahorse are all interesting prestige items for young biologists to own. A bagful of assorted shells would be a useful gift to offer a small child for sorting and counting or to offer an older child for collage work. Large shells make exciting stocking fillers for very young children. They will be able to hold them to their ears and listen to the sea.

An egg-shaped pebble can be turned into a golden egg. Let children paint a large one, to make a door stop, or a small one can make a paperweight. A large pebble can be painted with simple pictures or faces with acrylic paint. Varnish the finished design to preserve it.

A large shell or a small piece of driftwood can be used among dried flower arrangements, or you can drill a hole in a large piece of driftwood for arranging the flowers in.

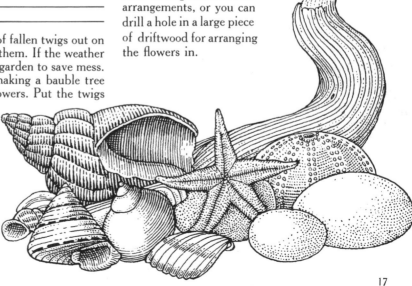

THE CHRISTMAS TREE

St Boniface was an English priest and was sent as a missionary to Northern Germany. One night as he was passing through a forest he came upon a group of pagans. They were celebrating a pagan festival around a great oak tree which was one of their gods. They had prepared the sacrifice of a young boy to the great oak tree. St Boniface was enraged. He snatched an axe from the nearest man and chopped down the oak. The boy was saved. Then St Boniface noticed a small spruce growing among the roots of the great oak. 'Let this small evergreen tree be your symbol of everlasting life,' said St Boniface. From that day onwards the spruce became the tree which formed the focal point of the Christmas celebrations in Northern Germany.

A Christmas tree in every home is a relatively recent innovation in the British Isles. At one time an arrangement of holly served as the main centrepiece in the home. There is a report of a Christmas tree being seen in a London street in the fifteenth century; however, the honour for the introduction of the first Christmas tree in Britain goes to Prince Albert. He imported a tree from his homeland of Germany for the royal children at Windsor Castle, and by the late 1840s it became a fashion and has now become a tradition. Today the Christmas tree is a worldwide symbol of Christmas in every Christian country.

Long ago it was the custom for the parents of a family to bring the tree indoors—usually on Christmas Eve—and to arrange the decorations and to light the candles whilst the children waited all agog in another room. The children were then shown the decorated tree as a wonderful surprise. Today it's one of our better customs to enlist the help of our children in decorating the tree. For a child the world is a 'don't touch' kind of place. At the very least the Christmas tree is one natural plant children can feel and touch and smell. A Christmas tree really is special magic—so big, so green and so full of promise. And what a gargantuan task it can be for a small child to help settle a tree into its tub!

PRESERVING A TREE WITH ROOTS

It would be worthwhile investing in a small tree with roots which can be used from year to year. Large trees usually die when they're transplanted but small trees stand a better chance.

Use a large garden tub. Line the bottom with broken crocks or pebbles to make good drainage. Fill the tub with a mixture of leaf mould or peat and garden soil. Leave the tree outside in the cool until the last possible moment on Christmas Eve. Once it's brought indoors give the tree a daily feed with ice cubes. These will melt slowly helping to keep the tree cool and moist. Stand the tree well away from any heating appliances and in the coolest place. Decorate the tub by wrapping it with silver foil or wrapping paper. Or make a tree skirt out of a circle of red or green felt.

As soon as Christmas decorations are taken down put the tree outside again. The tree should survive for the following Christmas providing it's given a drink in very hot weather. A small Christmas tree will grow quite comfortably in a tub on a patio or a balcony.

DECORATING THE TREE

Large silver baubles These are easy for very young children to make if the card cutting is done for them by an adult. Take a paper towel centre and slice it up like a Swiss roll. Make all the sections the same size. Wrap each section with silver foil, covering it inside and out. If the wrapping is wrinkled it helps to reflect the light. Take one ring and slide it at right angles inside another. Thread a cone or a large glass bead inside the bauble and through the top for hanging the bauble on to the Christmas tree.

Choirs of angels Collect together stiff card, a little gold or silver card, a ball of white wool, scraps of coloured wool, scissors, needle and cotton, glue and shirring elastic. Cut out a piece of stiff card, $2\frac{3}{8}''$ x $1\frac{1}{2}''$. Wind the wool on lengthways until the card is well covered. Slip off the card lengthways and pinch the wool together in the centre. Hold it tightly and stitch firmly $\frac{3}{8}''$ and $1\frac{3}{8}''$ down from the top to make the head and body.

To make both arms, cut out a small piece of card, $1\frac{1}{4}''$ x $\frac{3}{4}''$. Wind wool lengthways until the card is covered. Remove from card and sew hands $\frac{1}{4}''$ from each end. Split the body and push through the

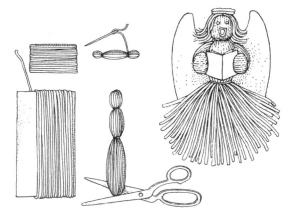

centre of the body with points of scissors until the arms extend equally out on either side.

To finish off: cut the bottom open to create a skirt. Embroider a face with coloured wool, and tie a gold thread around the waist. Cut out and glue on a tiny halo and a pair of wings. Suspend the angel by threading a loop of shirring elastic through the top of the head. For additional interest glue a tiny hymn book into the hands of each angel.

The fairy angel The northern Europeans once believed that the evergreens held the woodland spirits when the other trees of the forest were dead, and the angel on the tree has become a combined symbol of the ancient woodland spirit and the angels around the stable.

Any dainty plastic doll can be dressed for the tree. Unless the fairy is given a very special dress, the doll can be dressed afresh every year.

The bodice is easy because the doll will be fixed to the tallest spike of the tree so her dress can be backless. Just take a strip of material and cross it over the chest to fit inside the waistband of the skirt.

The skirt should stand out. Use any fine fabric like net curtain material or scraps of silk. Cut out a circle by drawing round a tea plate. Cut a small hole in the centre and slide the body through.

Allow children to scallop, fringe or decorate in any way they like.

Crêpe streamers Buy a flat packet of white crêpe paper. One packet will be sufficient for a fairly tall tree. Unfold it once and cut it along the longest edge to make thin strips. Let children unravel the snowy white streamer and loop it from spike to spike on the Christmas tree. Complete the decorations with a silver foil star at the top of the tree.

sides of the card. Hold the wound wool firmly and slip it off the card. Wind the sewing thread around the centre two or three times and knot. Cut open the ends of the bauble. Leave a long piece of sewing thread for suspending the bauble from the tree.

To make tassels, wind coloured crochet wool over three fingers several times. Hold the wool firmly and slide it off the fingers. Sew the top of the tassel and chop open the base. These can be used for decorating parcels as well as making tassels to suspend from the Christmas tree.

A spider's web Glue three cocktail sticks into a star shape. Leave them to set firmly. Beginning in the centre, using any silky thread, twist the thread around each stick twice to keep the shape firm. Leave a long piece for suspending from the tree. The finished web can be dipped in glue and glitter to give it a frosty appearance.

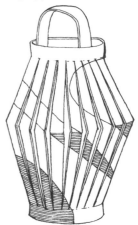

Egg shells Pierce the pointed end of an egg with a needle to allow the air in. Crack a large hole in the flattest end and clear away the tiny pieces of shell. Break the white and yolk inside the egg to make them run out together. Rinse inside the shells and leave them to drain.

Knot one end of a piece of shirring elastic. Place the knot inside the eggshell with the other end poked through the hole. Fix it in place on the outside with some green crêpe paper or green foil leaves, with a rubber solution glue. Decorate the shells with tiny beads, sequins, lace, coloured nail varnish, glitter or paint. Reinforce the finished shell with a coat of clear nail varnish.

Golden baubles and tassels Wind a length of gold or silver crochet wool over and over on a piece of card about 2″ x 4″. Sew the centre firmly on both

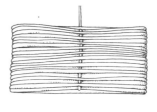

Lanterns Use the front of bright birthday and Christmas cards. Fold the card firmly in half. Fold a margin of $\frac{1}{3}''$ at the top and another at the base. Fringe the card finely from the centre to the margins. Open out the card and paste the ends of the strips. Paste on a strip of card for the handle and hang on the tree.

THE NATIONAL BIRD OF THE BRITISH ISLES

The robin has been given official status quite recently. He didn't need it. He's surrounded with legends and has appeared on Christmas cards from the very start.

The robin is easy to recognize by the red flash down his breast and can often be seen hopping about alone in the garden. In the British Isles he is one of the few birds which doesn't migrate.

When a robin is shown hospitality he will visit the same house regularly. He is quite fearless of humans. In the Middle Ages people suspected he must be the familiar of witches, and it was considered most unwise to gossip in the presence of a robin. If an old lady gave crusts to a robin she soon found herself with an unfortunate reputation.

SAINTS AND SINNERS

When good people died they became saints and went up to heaven. When bad people died, as sin-

ners, they were thrown into the fiery depths of hell. The robin was a sympathetic little bird. When he heard about the sinners he flew down to hell. It distressed the robin to hear the sinners screaming for water, so he flew back to earth and collected a skin full of water and returned to the fiery depths. The fierce flames beat him back. The brave little robin tried again and again to fly into the burning fire. The water evaporated and the poor little bird scorched his breast. That is why the robin has a red breast.

THE ROBIN AND THE CROSS

The robin heard about Christ's Crucifixion and flew to Jerusalem. The journey took several days. By the time the robin arrived Christ was dying on the Cross. The poor little robin flew down to the Cross in an attempt to ease Christ's pain. There was nothing he could do. A few drops of Christ's blood spilled down the robin's breast. That is why the robin has a red breast.

In Victorian times the postmen wore red jackets and acquired the nickname of 'Robin'. It's uncertain which came first, the robin on the Christmas card or the postman nicknamed 'Robin' who delivered the card.

HOW FIRE WAS BROUGHT TO EARTH

All the birds of the air quarrelled. They couldn't decide which bird should rule as king. It was agreed to settle the dispute by competition. The bird who flew highest would be acclaimed as the king of all the birds.

The birds flew up into the sky. The cunning little wren sat on the eagle's back. Gradually the smaller, weaker birds dropped out of the race. Finally only the eagle was left with the tiny wren on his back. At last, even the mighty eagle began to tire, so the wren flew on up towards the sun. When the wren reached the sun his wings caught fire. He plummeted down to earth with burning wings, bringing fire to man. As the wren was dying all the birds of the air declared him the king of the birds. The robin threw himself on to his friend in an attempt to put out the flames, but the wren died and the robin scorched his breast. And that is why man has fire; why the wren is the king of the birds and why the robin has a red breast.

A HAPPY CHRISTMAS

CHRISTMAS CARDS

Before Roland Hill introduced the penny postage rate in 1840, it had been the custom for families to write to absent members of the family sending news and seasonal compliments at Christmas. With the introduction of the penny post a half rate was specified for unsealed envelopes and postcards. This made it economically possible for many more families to communicate with each other.

The first Christmas card can be attributed to John Halcott Horsley, who was commissioned in 1843 by Sir Henry Cole to design a card he could

send to friends and members of his family. The end product was a hand-coloured lithograph which said 'A merry Christmas and a Happy New Year to You'.

The idea slowly caught on. Many Christmas cards began as writing paper enhanced with Christmas symbols. Later cards were sold in sheets of a dozen to be cut out and hand finished by the sender. Folded cards became fashionable and eventually the fashion swept the whole Christian world.

Homemade cards can look very amateurish. To avoid disappointment read through the following list of general hints:

1 Use a pair of really sharp scissors, a ruler and a set square. Crooked lines show up badly.
2 Measure accurately.
3 Use paste or glue sparingly and allow to dry naturally or it may buckle.
4 Score folds firmly with a sharp fingernail or a blunt pencil.
5 Use a soft lead pencil for marking and use it lightly.
6 Use the right glue or paste for the work. For example, silver foil isn't easy to stick down with a water-based paste. Rubber solution glue needs to be used sparingly or it oozes out over the finished work.

7 Never paste stiff pictures of card on to card The effect is crude.

WRITING THE MESSAGE

Lettering is one of the most difficult skills to acquire. It certainly can't be learned in one quick evening session. Tracing can be a safe method, but it involves hours of tedious work.

The effect of beautiful handwork on a Christmas card can be ruined with a poorly written message. Old people sometimes have wonderful handwriting which is charmingly full of pothooks and hangers and it has a look of antiquity in our ballpoint age. In return for a favour (such as a load of heavy shopping) ask an elderly person with beautiful writing to inscribe the messages on your Christmas cards. Have the messages written on cards before any artwork is put on to them. This will prevent any worries about making blots on a finished card.

If you don't know anyone who can write for you then follow one of the simple suggestions listed below:

1 Use a mapping pen and indian ink. Write using very small letters.
2 Use a thick felt pen and make the message really bold.
3 Cut out a stencilled message. Dab over it with thick paint using either a stencil brush or an old toothbrush.
4 Dip a length of coloured thread into paste. Press the message on using the thread.
5 Paste the message and dip it into glitter.

SIMPLE CHRISTMAS CARDS

Press three holly leaves for a few days until they are quite flat. Coat them with clear nail varnish. Arrange and glue the leaves on to a card. Tie on a red ribbon at the corner. Dot on a few painted holly berries. Or, arrange three pressed holly leaves on a card and stencil over the edges using an old

toothbrush. Dot on some holly berries with a felt-tipped pen.

Press some pieces of common woodland fern. Arrange them on a card. Splash over the ferns with diluted green watercolour paint using an old toothbrush.

Wild flowers, leaves and ferns can be made into delicate Christmas cards and gift tags. A greeting card with an arrangement of wild flowers would be very touching for a friend living abroad. Set the flowers on the card in the same way as for picture

making with garden flowers. Use a mapping pen and indian ink to write a description. For example the description might say 'Buttercups and Daisies From a Meadow Beside the Cam', or 'Wild Forget-Me-Nots from Church Lane'.

Lace doily. Take dark paper for the base of the card and fold it. Fold a sheet of white paper twice and then once diagonally. Snip out a decorative edge and along the sections. Unfold and paste on to the card base. Iron out the creases if necessary with a cool iron.

Wax relief. Draw a Christmas picture on to the front of folded white paper, using a stub of white wax candle. Cover this with a thin coat of water-based paint.

String card. Select a Christmas greeting or symbol and pencil it on to the front of folded paper. Glue a length of string on to the markings, pressing down firmly as you go.

Explosive greeting. Write the chosen greeting with thick black felt pen, and zig-zag around the word with strong colours, finishing with bright yellow.

Blackmail message. Chop individual letters from newspapers or magazines. Paste each letter and stick it into place on a card.

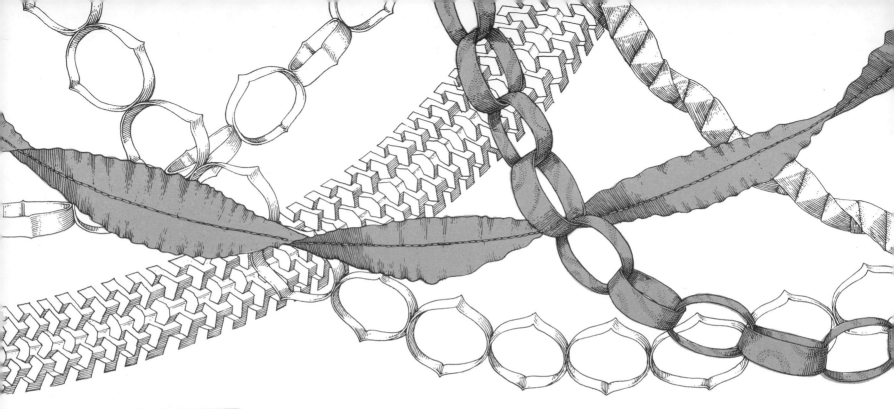

PAPER DECORATIONS

PAPER CHAINS

Packets of paper chains with gummed edges can be bought in the stationer's shop, but the colours can be dreary. Instead try using brightly coloured paper bags, wrapping paper or coloured gummed squares. Cut them into strips and paste them into links. Snowy paper chains which have been snipped into lace patterns can look enchanting. Fold them for pattern making but iron out the creases before pasting.

Delicate garlands can be made from tissues, although they are more difficult. Cut out strips of coloured paper or crêpe paper 2″ x 4″. Fold a strip lengthways twice, folding sides to centre. Cut into the centre by snipping, like fringing, alternate sides, then unfold. Thin coloured paper can also be used instead of tissue to make these garlands.

Children enjoy making zigzag chains although they don't always hang well, but they can be suspended instead of looped.

Cut out two long strips of coloured paper about half an inch wide. Paste the ends firmly together at right angles. Fold over and over, pressing the work down firmly, keeping it flat. Paste the last two squares together to hold the whole paper chain in place.

It is possible to make chains so that they can be stored. Use a piece of thin paper which is coloured

30

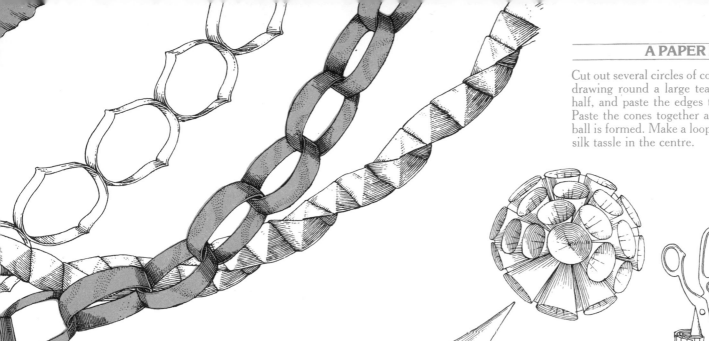

A PAPER BAUBLE

Cut out several circles of coloured tissue or paper by drawing round a large tea cup. Cut each circle in half, and paste the edges together to make a cone. Paste the cones together at the points until a large ball is formed. Make a loop for hanging by pasting a silk tassle in the centre.

A PAPER TREE

Cover a cotton reel with silver foil, leaving the hole in the top open. Use a length of crêpe paper as wide as a handspan and as long as the distance from the tip of the nose to the tip of an outstretched arm. Roll the strip of paper. Fringe it deeply, and gently pull the centre upwards. Press the boughs down firmly.

Place on top a three-dimensional star: fold paper in four and cut out two stars.

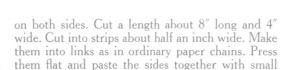

on both sides. Cut a length about 8″ long and 4″ wide. Cut into strips about half an inch wide. Make them into links as in ordinary paper chains. Press them flat and paste the sides together with small dabs of paste in the centre.

To store, press flat and place elastic bands at the end.

For criss-cross chains, use the same method but paste each link together crossed alternately.

PAPER STREAMERS

To make paper streamers, use a packet of coloured crêpe paper. Cut out a broad strip. Use a sewing machine to run a straight line down the centre, gathering as you go. Fringe the edges.

CHRISTMAS CRACKERS

The story of the first Christmas cracker is one which happens to be true.

Tom Smith was a confectioner living in London in 1840. On a business trip to France he was intrigued with the sugared almonds which were sold in twists of tissue paper. The French called them 'Bon-bons'. They were exchanged as gifts between adults.

Tom Smith was fascinated with the idea because sweets were always sold unwrapped and lacked any value as novelties. He began importing 'Bon-bons' from France. Tom Smith's sales of sweets increased, and he improved on the basic French idea by wrapping the sweets in brightly coloured twists of paper. Later still he improved them by including love mottoes inside the wrapping, like the fortune cookies which American children enjoy.

Being a man of great initiative Tom Smith then replaced the sugared almonds with toys and novelties. The new invention didn't catch on as he had hoped. Tom Smith was despondent but not defeated. He sat before his log fire on Christmas Day

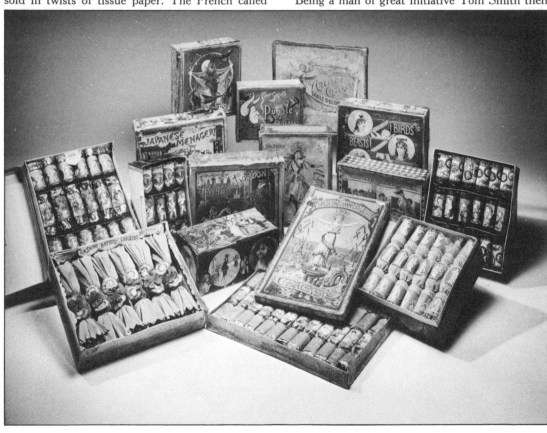

pondering the problem. He stretched out his foot and turned a log with his shoe. Immediately the log spurted out a jet of flame. There was a small popping explosion as hot resin from the burning log ignited.

Crack, pop, crackle went the log. Tom Smith knew at once that he had found the missing ingredient for his Bon-bons. After many experiments he succeeded in making the snap for the log-shaped paper cracker. The Christmas cracker quickly became established as a novel addition to Christmas parties.

At Tom Smith's factory, which is still in existence in Norfolk, over a thousand people work in the manufacture of Christmas crackers all the year round.

Thirteen million are produced annually and a hundred tons of cardboard are used for making the cracker boxes. One skilled cracker maker can make 160,000 crackers in a year, even allowing time off for holidays! Five tons of cardboard are used for making the bangs, known in the trade as detonators, and twenty tons of glue and paste are mixed annually.

> The largest ever made was 45 feet long and 8 feet in diameter, built for the BBC 'Record Breakers' Show' on 27th December 1974.
> *Guiness Book of Records, 1978*

The detonators in crackers are the most essential ingredient. Since it's illegal to sell gunpowder, in any form, it's impossible to make crackers which resemble the genuine product. Try buying the cheapest crackers, just to obtain the detonators and decorated cases. Replace the contents with cheap but interesting novelties.

Squeakers and whizzers and suchlike bought from the novelty counter of a chain store give good value. Children who are good at corny jokes can help with refurbishing the crackers by writing out jokes and mottoes—at the very least some of the spellings might be funny. To repack crackers tightly, take a piece of string and pull it round the open end of crackers using a looseknot.

Crackers make excellent presents for the winners of family party games. One box goes a long way and even then the winner isn't certain of the prize unless he wins the contents of the cracker.

CRACKER JOKES

These are usually awful, because they are written with the aim of not giving offence—consequently they don't make anyone laugh either. Inventive children can make up better jokes than the cracker makers dare publish.

Riddles are popular and can be read out for the whole family to answer. For example:

Why does the queen wear red, white and blue garters?
To keep her socks up.

What is the difference between an elephant and a letterbox?
Remind me not to send you to post a letter!

What game do spacemen play on their way to the moon?
Astronauts and crosses.

And then there are the really daft riddles:

What is slim and red and about a foot long and crosses the Atlantic at 500 m.p.h.?
Supersonic rhubarb.

What isn't a cat but has whiskers, paws, fur and a tail?
A kitten!

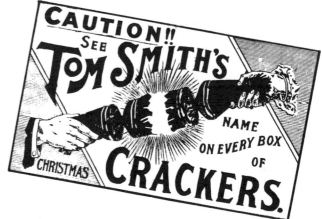

ADVENT CALENDARS

These must be one of the finest seasonal items for children to make. From the first day of December until Christmas Eve they open a little window each day, counting off the days until Christmas Day arrives at last.

Advent calendars are very easy to make. Use one sheet of firm card for the base, and thinner card for the cover. Cut out tiny pictures from old Christmas cards or copy the drawings on this page. Mark the base card with ruled lines. Do the same, faintly, to the cover card. Pencil a Christmas tree, a snow-covered house or any other seasonal picture on the cover card. Arrange the twenty-four pictures on the base card, and mark the cover card with numbers to correspond. Place a ruler beside each square on the cover card and prick one side several times with a pin to make a perforated line. Thread a ribbon through each window to make it easy to open. Paper staples can be used instead of ribbon.

Paste on the cover card and paint the drawing; cover abundantly with glitter.

STAINED-GLASS WINDOWS

Draw a seasonal design to scale on paper before starting work on the real window. Children who aren't too confident about using a design of their own may need to copy from a Christmas card.

Working on anything as potentially messy as stained glass windows will need firm rules laid down before children begin. If children smudge any paint into cracks in woodwork around the windowsill it will be difficult to remove. Smear a little neat liquid detergent over the window woodwork and leave it there until the work is finished. Spread out plenty of newspaper on the windowsill and below the window.

Use thick black poster or powder paint for the lead outlines, and make these first. Then transfer the coloured areas using the design on the paper section by section. Real stained glass windows glow in deep jewel colours, so try to keep to deeper colours for the most traditional effect. If the design isn't quite big enough to fill the window finish off the edges by making tiny squares of colour around the edge just as the ancient makers of stained glass windows did.

PART II

CAROLS AND CAROLLING

Here we come a-wassailing,
Among the leaves so green,
Here we come a-wandering,
So fair to be seen.

soon realized the rewards of carol singing and became carollers themselves.

'Wassail, wassail, all over the town' chants the old carol, and this is what our great-great-grandparents did, collecting pennies, sweet-meats, rosy red apples, mince pies and handfuls of nuts as they went.

'Wassail' was a greeting in old English which means, 'Be of good cheer'. At one time the wassail bowl stood in every home, and householders would hand out a drink from the bowl to anyone who served them throughout the year.

Although we give money instead of wassail now, we can still enjoy a Christmas drink.

Put half a pint of ale, a little ginger, a clove, a small piece of butter and a teaspoonful of sugar into a pan and bring the mixture to the boil. Beat up two eggs with a tablespoonful of cold ale, pour the boiling ale into the egg mixture and then into a large jug. Pour the contents rapidly from one large jug to another a few times, then return the liquor to the pan and heat it again to nearly boiling point. Serve the ale very hot.

CAROL SINGING

In Great Grandmother Conway's house it was the custom to stoke up a huge log on the evening of Christmas Eve. The whole family would sit around the fire roasting chestnuts and singing carols. If carol singers called at the door they went cheerfully away with a few pennies and a pocketful of hot chestnuts.

There can be few more perfect opportunities to sing carols than on Christmas Eve. For many people carol singing is the only form of community singing they experience throughout the year.

MUMMERS

The mummers were the first to sing carols. They were groups of wandering actors who travelled from town to town, acting out Bible stories to the gentry and peasants who couldn't read. As part of the play acting carols were sung, and these took the form of Easter and summer songs as well as those for Christmas.

The earliest carol of which we have a record was a summer one, 'Summer is a-Coming In'; through the course of time most summer and Easter carols have been lost, though there is still an abundance of Christmas carols.

Musical instruments in the Middle Ages had a limited range of notes and therefore the old traditional carols are easy to recognize for their limited range of notes. Even today, they sound as perfect when they're played on a penny whistle as when they're played on an organ.

The mummers were rewarded for their performances as they toured the towns and villages. The tradition was handed on to children as they

RULES FOR CAROLLERS

It is best to organize local children into a large group rather than to let them go out in groups of two or three. Some householders get annoyed by the constant ringing of the doorbell, and children in a small group can't create enough volume to make themselves heard.

There are a few rules which young carol singers must know before they set out:
1. Never go into any house; friends and neighbours always understand the good sense of this.
2. Never trample on flower beds.

3. Ring a doorbell only once (although you can give it one long hard ring).
4. Remember your manners. Always say 'Merry Christmas' and 'thank you' when given a gift of money or sweets.
5. Never start a quarrel or fight on someone's doorstep.
6. Always give good value and sing several carols—but don't outstay your welcome.

If the carollers plan to collect for a charity they should contact the charity once they have decided on one. Most charities will be pleased to supply collection tins if they have advance warning.

By far the most important point is that the carollers know the words of the songs and know which ones they can sing. It is far better for them to learn two songs thoroughly than to attempt an ambitious programme. It helps if children rehearse several times and have a trial run at their own front door before they set

off. It is a good idea to take song sheets along; even if children aren't fluent readers, a carol book will give a shy child something to focus on, and those sure of the words can keep the singing going.

A LANTERN-BEARER

A lantern not only brings the singers closer to their predecessors, the early mummers, but it also adds a touch of magic, with its warm, re-assuring glow. Cut a lantern out of stiff card. Tie a torch inside it, and then tie it to a strong twig or broomstick.

AWAY IN A MANGER

This carol is called 'Luther's Cradle Hymn', There is no record of Martin Luther writing any carols, though perhaps it was his favourite carol.

Whether Martin Luther wrote it or not, it is certainly the carol which most captures the spirit of Christmas.

Away in a manger, no crib for a bed,
The little Lord Jesus laid down his sweet head.
The stars in the bright sky looked down where
  He lay,
The little Lord Jesus asleep on the hay.

The cattle are lowing, the Baby awakes,
But little Lord Jesus no crying He makes.
I love Thee, Lord Jesus! Look down from the
  sky,
And stay by my bedside until morning is nigh.

Be near me, Lord Jesus; I ask Thee to stay
Close by me for ever, and love me, I pray.
Bless all the dear children in Thy tender care,
And fit us for Heaven, to live with Thee there.

The source of the Coventry can be traced to the earliest lullabyes. An Anglo-Irish friar recorded 'Lolloi, lolloi, litel child' as long ago as 1315. By 1372 the lolloi had become 'Lullay, lullay, litel child, softe slep and faste', and was recorded by John de Grimstone. We are grateful to the anonymous Anglo-Irish friar and to John de Grimstone that our children can learn to sing this beautiful lullabye carol six hundred years later.

Herod the king in his raging
Charged he hath this day
His men of might in his own sight,
All children young to slay.

Then woe is me, poor Child, for Thee!
and ever, morn and day,
For Thy parting nor say nor sing
Bye, bye, lullay, lullay.

Lullay, Thou little tiny child,
Bye, bye, lullay, lullay,
Lullay, Thou little tiny child,
Bye, bye, lullay, lullay.

Oh sisters, too, how may we do?
For to preserve this day,
This poor Youngling, for whom we sing
Bye, bye, lullay, lullay.

HERE WE COME A-WASSAILING

This traditional old English carol set the scene for carol singing from door to door. It originated from mummers and children adapted it for their own needs. The words can sound ridiculous if the carol is sung anywhere but on a neighbour's doorstep.

Here we come a-wassailing, among the leaves so green,
Here we come a-wandering, so fair to be seen.
Love and joy come to you, and to you your wassail too,
And God bless you, and send you a happy New Year,
And God send you a happy New Year.

We are not daily beggars, that beg from door to door,
But we are neighbours' children whom you have seen before.

Chorus

We have got a little purse of stretching leather skin;
We want a little money to line it well within.

Chorus

God bless the master of this house, likewise the mistress too;
And all the little children that round the table go.

Chorus

WE WISH YOU A MERRY CHRISTMAS

This is one of the easiest carols for very young children to learn. They can sing it with actions, including an emphatic stamp of the foot, on the line, 'We won't go until we get some'. It's easy to understand how this carol was kept alive: it was composed by mummers and the good strong rhythm and cheerful greeting ensured its endurance.

We wish you a merry Christmas,
We wish you a merry Christmas,
We wish you a merry Christmas and a happy
  New Year.

Chorus
Good tidings we bring to you and your king.
We wish you a merry Christmas and a happy
  New Year.

We all want some figgy pudding,
We all want some figgy pudding,
We all want some figgy pudding, so bring some
  out here!

Chorus

We won't go until we get some,
We won't go until we get some,
We won't go until we get some, so bring some
  out here!

Chorus

We wish you a merry Christmas,
We wish you a merry Christmas,
We wish you a merry Christmas, and a happy
  New Year.

THE HOLLY AND THE IVY

Christmas wouldn't be complete without this beautiful old English carol which tells the legend of the holly tree. The words are easy to learn and remember because the verses tell of the natural seasons of the holly tree.

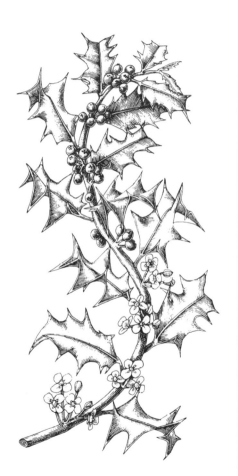

The holly and the ivy, now both are well full grown,
Of all the trees that are in the wood, the holly bears the crown,
The rising of the sun, and the running of the deer,
The playing of the merry organ, sweet singing in the choir.

The holly bears a blossom, as white as any flow'r,
And Mary bore sweet Jesus Christ, to be our sweet Saviour.
The rising of the sun, and the running of the deer,
The playing of the merry organ, sweet singing in the choir.

The holly bears a berry, as red as any blood,
And Mary bore sweet Jesus Christ, to do poor sinners good.
The rising of the sun, and the running of the deer,
The playing of the merry organ, sweet singing in the choir.

The holly bears a prickle, as sharp as any thorn,
And Mary bore sweet Jesus Christ, on Christmas Day in the morn.
The rising of the sun, and the running of the deer,
The playing of the merry organ, sweet singing in the choir.

I SAW THREE SHIPS COME SAILING BY

This old traditional English carol began as a song about the three ships of the desert: the wise men on their camels. The words changed through usage to visual images which ordinary folk could comprehend.

I saw three ships come sailing by
On Christmas Day, on Christmas Day,
I saw three ships come sailing by
On Christmas Day in the morning.

And who was in those ships all three,
Ships all three, ships all three?
And who was in those ships all three
On Christmas Day in the morning?

Our Jesus Christ and His Lady,
His Lady, His Lady.
Our Jesus Christ and His Lady
On Christmas Day in the morning.

And all the bells on earth shall ring
On Christmas Day, on Christmas Day.
And all the bells on earth shall ring
On Christmas Day in the morning.

And you will whistle and I will sing
On Christmas Day, on Christmas Day.
And you will whistle and I will sing
On Christmas Day in the morning.

DECK THE HALLS

It was impossible to make a short selection of Christmas carols without including this beautiful Welsh ringing carol. 'Druids' still live in Wales; as children decorate their homes with greenery and sing this merry carol they have a very firm link with their Welsh cousins.

Deck the halls with boughs of holly,
Fa la la la la la la la la.
'Tis the season to be jolly,
Fa la la la la la la la la.
Don we now our gay apparel,
Fa la la la la la la la la.
Troll the ancient Yuletide carol,
Fa la la la la la la la la.

See the blazing Yule before us,
Fa la la la la la la la la.
Strike the harp and join the chorus,
Fa la la la la la la la la.
Follow me in merry measure,
Fa la la la la la la la la.
While I tell of Yuletide treasure,
Fa la la la la la la la la.

Fast away the old year passes,
Fa la la la la la la la la.
Fail the new ye lads and lasses,
Fa la la la la la la la la.
Sing we joyous altogether,
Fa la la la la la la la la.
Heedless of the wind and weather,
Fa la la la la la la la la.

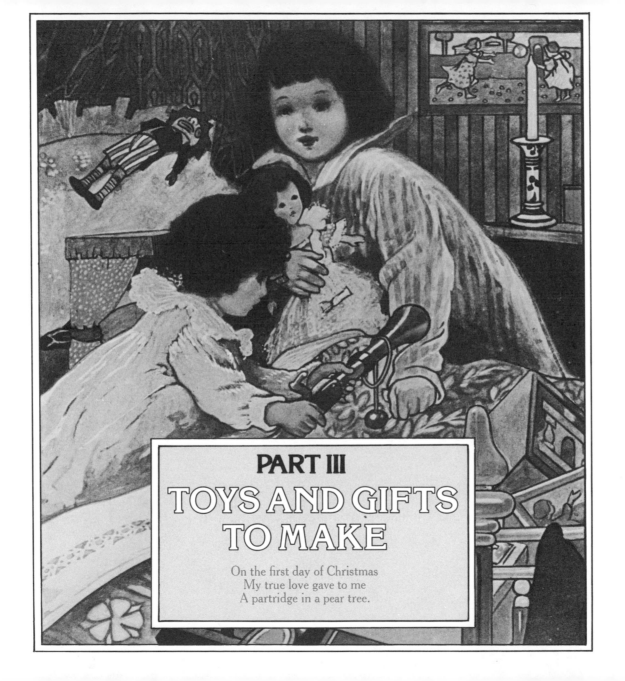

PART III

TOYS AND GIFTS
TO MAKE

On the first day of Christmas
My true love gave to me
A partridge in a pear tree.

TRADITIONAL TOYS

It's a relatively modern custom to give children toys as gifts for Christmas. Before 1900 only privileged children enjoyed commercially made toys, and many of these were handmade, such as dolls, rocking horses, carts, forts and lead soldiers. The majority of children would receive little novelties of sweetmeats, ribbons, charcoal, paper novelties and perhaps a homemade doll or sailor boy.

During the second half of the nineteenth century all children received a basic education. This increased the demand for printed material of every kind, and the manufacturers began catering for a mass market. Toys such as jigsaw puzzles, picture books and board games became widely available by the turn of the century.

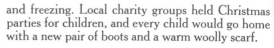

Older people may still remember Christmas at the turn of the century. The local benefactor would arrive at the school to distribute gifts to all the children. These were rubber balls, skipping ropes, five stones, purses, necklaces of glass beads, little wooden soldiers, miniature parasoles, packets of Japanese paper flowers which magically unfolded in water, fans, windmills and cellophane birds which spiralled down a twist of wire.

'Penny plain and tuppence coloured' were popular with children a hundred years ago. They were sheets of card, with the outline of various London theatres on each. Actors and actresses came dressed for the part as stick puppets. Penny plains meant a lot of work colouring, but for tuppence, they came all ready to cut out and put together.

Toys had to be abandoned during the recession of the hungry thirties. The children were starving

and freezing. Local charity groups held Christmas parties for children, and every child would go home with a new pair of boots and a warm woolly scarf.

Just as the recession was ending Europe was thrown into the Second World War. The reviving toy factories became munition factories. All parents rich and poor alike were thrown back on to their own resources. Fathers hammered and chiselled and painted and went back to making the traditional toys such as building blocks, wagons, pull-a-long ducks and sailing boats. Mothers knitted and sewed. The soft toys made from unravelled outgrown jumpers had an especially suitable curly texture. Anyone who was a child in the early 1940s will remember their handmade toys with affection. (My mother wasn't a great needlewoman, but the black doll made from a scrap of black-out material, with two brass curtain rings for earrings and a red bandana will always be remembered.)

Now we are in the age of plastic toys. Durable, with vivid colours, thoughtful design, constant new ideas, endless selection and mass produced, we have now gone full circle where all children can enjoy the quality of play.

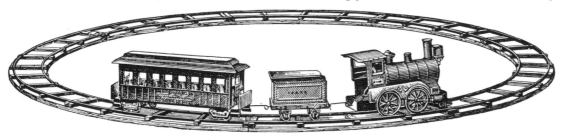

ST NICHOLAS

It seems certain that Nicholas, the patron saint of children, travellers and many others, was a fifth-century bishop of Myra, in Turkey. It is said that he was a very rich man who liked to help people anonymously, and his charitable acts became legendary. The date of his death, 6 December, is one of the few things known about him, which is the day now celebrated as St Nicholas's Day.

One of the best-known stories about him is 'St Nicholas and the Christmas Stocking'.

ST NICHOLAS AND THE CHRISTMAS STOCKING

A poor peasant had three beautiful daughters. Without the means to provide his daughters with a dowry, the peasant was forced to make plans to sell them into slavery.

The time came for the eldest daughter to be sold. That night a bag of gold coins was thrown through the open window. The peasant used the gold coins as a dowry for the eldest daughter and she was saved from slavery.

Soon plans had to be made to sell the second daughter. This time a bag of gold coins was thrown through the open window, and it landed right in a stocking hanging by the fire to dry. Now the second daughter could use the bag of gold coins as her dowry.

The peasant was puzzled. He was determined to discover the identity of the generous benefactor who had called in the night. When the time came for the peasant to make plans to sell his youngest daughter into slavery, he prayed that the visitor would call again. He kept a nightly vigil so that he could meet and thank this mysterious person.

Nicholas, the good bishop, came in the dark of night and tossed a third bag of gold coins through the window. The peasant identified him and told everyone of the bishop's kindness.

This is where the custom of children hanging up their stockings before Christmas originated. Children in some parts of the world still hang up their stockings on 5 December, the eve of St Nicholas, and when the feast day was put off to 25 December, this custom transferred with it.

As late as 1840 St Nicholas was depicted as a thin, gaunt old man, usually wearing black robes, a crown of holly and carrying a staff. The Victorians adopted him as a 'spirit of Christmas' and showed him as a more jolly figure, drinking wine and inviting people to 'make merry'. Dutch settlers in America brought with them their Santa Claus

(St Nicholas—Sinter Claes), and gradually we have come to see him as rounder of figure, dressed in scarlet clothes and carrying a sack filled with toys. This picture of him was immortalized in 1822 by Dr Clement Clarke Moore in his poem, 'The Night Before Christmas'.

For more than a hundred years this poem has charmed and delighted children. Dr Moore, an American professor of Greek literature, wrote it for the amusement of his own children with no intention of publishing it. The poem was copied and appeared anonymously in the *Troy Sentinel*, a newspaper of Troy, New York, in 1823. The scholar has been forgotten, and today Dr Clement Clarke Moore is only remembered for his simple and popular poem.

The figure depicted by Moore was popularized by the American cartoonist, Thomas Nast. His illustration of Father Christmas, which first appeared in *Harpers Weekly* in 1863, quickly spread to other artists and poets.

Thomas Nast's famous illustration of Santa Claus, as printed in *Christmas Poems*, 1863-64.

'Twas the night before Christmas, when all
    through the house
Not a creature was stirring, not even a mouse;
The stockings were hung by the chimney with care,
In hopes that St Nicholas soon would be there;
The children were nestled all snug in their beds,
While visions of sugar-plums danced in their heads;
And mamma in her kerchief, and I in my cap,
Had just settled our brains for a long winter's nap—

When out on the lawn there arose such a clatter,
I sprang from my bed to see what was the matter.
Away to the window I flew like a flash,
Tore open the shutters and threw up the sash.
The moon, on the breast of the new-fallen snow,
Gave a lustre of midday to objects below;
When what to my wondering eyes should appear
But a miniature sleigh and eight tiny reindeer,
With a little old driver, so lively and quick,
I knew in a moment it must be St Nick.

More rapid than eagles his coursers they came,
And he whistled and shouted, and called them by
    name:
'Now, Dasher! now, Dancer! now, Prancer and
    Vixen!
On, Comet! on, Cupid! on, Donder and Blitzen!
To the top of the porch, to the top of the wall!
Now, dash away, dash away all!'

From *The Night Before Christmas*, published by Porter and Coats in Philadelphia, 1883.

As dry leaves that before the wild hurricane fly,
When they meet with an obstacle, mount to the sky,
So, up to the house-top the coursers they flew,
With the sleigh full of toys—and St Nicholas too
And then in a twinkling I heard on the roof
The prancing and pawing of each little hoof.
As I drew in my head and was turning around,
Down the chimney St Nicholas came with a bound.
He was dressed all in fur from his head to his foot,
And his clothes were all tarnished with ashes and
　　soot;
A bundle of toys he had flung on his back,
And he looked like a peddler just opening his pack.

His eyes how they twinkled! his dimples how merry!
His cheeks were like roses, his nose like a cherry;
His droll little mouth was drawn up like a bow,
And the beard on his chin was as white as the snow.
The stump of his pipe he held in his teeth,
And the smoke it encircled his head like a wreath.
He had a broad face, and a little round belly
That shook, when he laughed, like a bowl full of
　　jelly.
He was chubby and plump,—a right jolly old elf—
And I laughed when I saw him, in spite of myself.

A wink of his eye and a twist of his head
Soon gave me to know I had nothing to dread.
He spoke not a word, but went straight to his work,
And filled all the stockings; then turned with a jerk,
And laying his finger aside of his nose,
And giving a nod, up the chimney he rose.
He sprang to his sleigh, to his team gave a whistle,
And away they all flew like the down of a thistle;
But I heard him exclaim, ere he drove out of sight:
'Happy Christmas to all, and to all a good-night!'

Katie in *What Katie Did* was a very clever girl. She wrote her letter to Father Christmas, placed it near the fire, and opened the door to create a draught. Consequently the letter flew straight up the chimney.

Sometimes children write letters to Father Christmas and post it to the North Pole. However, since Father Christmas doesn't live at the North Pole it is best if parents say they will post the letter for their children, and then keep it to help with buying presents.

When a child is too young to write, give him a sheet of paper and some crayons and ask him to draw his letter to Father Christmas. Children sometimes draw a picture of themselves for Father Christmas as well as drawing the things they would like in their stocking. Or, if the child is very young, ask him to scribble along the page, just as adults appear to do when they write. The child can say aloud what he is writing and a translation can be written on the back of the paper for future reference.

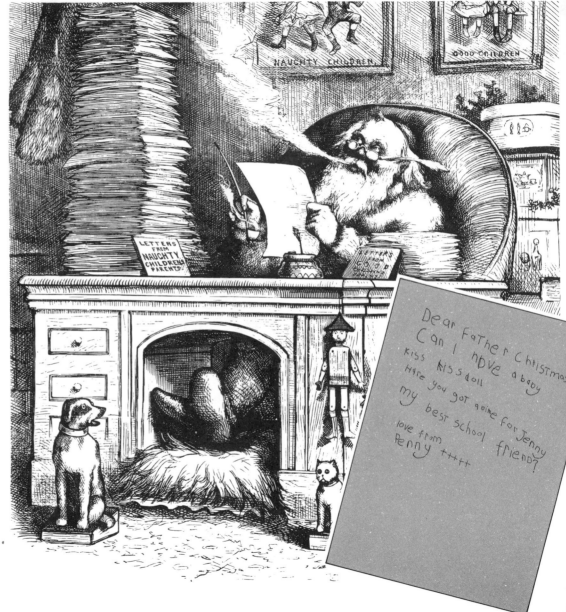

FILLING THE STOCKING

Very young children are interested in everything. Their play takes the form of exploration in many directions and with many and varied materials. A stockingful of books may be ideal for an older child who shows an obvious love of reading but for the young child the stocking should offer a little of everything.

TRADITIONAL SYMBOLS

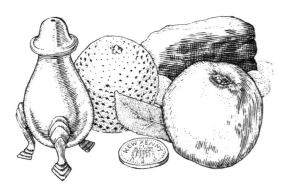

It has become customary to fill the toe of the stocking with a plump, rosy apple. It's there to offer health and happiness for the coming year. The heel of the stocking is traditionally filled with an orange. Until this century oranges were a luxury only the wealthy could afford.

Children were always assured of a prosperous future if they found a bright new penny, gleaming fresh from the mint, in the stocking. Old people remember the piece of coal, wrapped in tissue, which was always included in the contents of the stocking. The coal was a symbol of warmth, and it promised the child would be kept warm for the coming year. Salt was a vital commodity to our ancestors. It was precious for preserving food and was often used for trading. Roman soldiers were paid part of their wages in salt which is where the word 'salary' comes from. In the past children always found a piece of salt in their stocking for good luck.

The real skill of filling a stocking comes from knowing a particular child really well and in finding just the right toy or novelty. Every child, young or old, will find a use for a large sketchbook or scrapbook, even if they found one in their stocking last year. They are inexpensive and will give hours of play value on winter afternoons. A large plain-leaved book rolled up makes an excellent spine for filling the centre of the stocking. Add a small packet of crayons, a packet of felt pens or two lead pencils, one hard and one soft, for some experimental drawings.

A GOLDEN CROWN

On the day when children celebrate the birthday of the King of Heaven a golden crown makes a very appropriate gift to find in the stocking.

Measure the child's head carefully. Remember that children's heads are not much smaller than our own. It's always easier to make a large hat smaller than to increase the size of a too small paper hat. If several children are to receive golden crowns it will be important to make each one a slightly different shape or put names on them to avoid arguments over ownership.

Cut out the crown from stiff gold card. Fix it with strong glue and leave it to dry with paper clips or clothes pegs. Glue on gems taken from junk jewellery, sequins, gold and silver braid and broken costume jewellery.

A golden crown for the stocking need not be wrapped. Allow it to peek invitingly out of the top.

'THE DEVIL ON TWO STICKS'

As its name suggests a diabolo is devilishly difficult to work. To make a diabolo, take two long sticks and a length of fine, strong string the length of two outstretched arms. Fix either end of the string to ends of the sticks. Then fix two wooden discs at right angles to either end of a short dowel rod. To work a diabolo, hold the sticks outstretched, and balance the wooden reel on the string, running it back and forth.

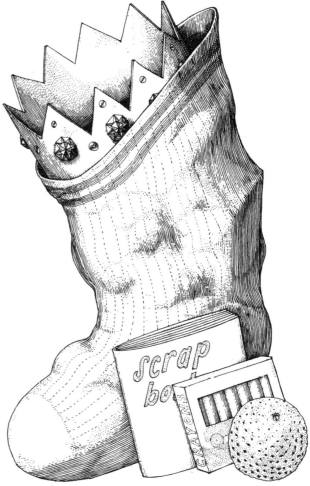

A BUZZER

Ancient buzzers are sometimes found on archaeological sites. They are usually made from a coin with two holes drilled through. To make a buzzer, use a large decorative button or a circle of decorated card. Pierce two holes if necessary. Thread it with a piece of string about the length of the child's outstretched arms. To work a buzzer, hold the loop of string without tension. Spin it over and over. Pull the string taut and release. Repeat to make a buzzing noise.

Another similar toy is a spinning novelty. Write out a message, like 'Happy Christmas' or a person's name, on a round piece of card, half on one side, and half on the other. String the card with two pieces of string which pass through two holes on opposite sides of the circle. When you spin the card, you will be able to see the whole of the message at once.

MUSICAL INSTRUMENTS

Music is one glorious facet of childhood which can be catered for in the Christmas stocking. Penny whistles, recorders, mouth organs and little plastic

bird whistles are all exciting items to find in the stocking. Homemade musical instruments can be just as thrilling.

Buy six small bells from the pet shop which are designed to go on the collars of dogs and cats. Buy six closed eyelets (the type used for hanging net curtains). Buy one thick piece of dowel rod. Paint the dowel rod a bright colour. Fix the bells into the eyelets, and screw the eyelets into the dowel rod.

To make maracas, use a firm plastic pot with a lid. Put in a few grains of rice, lentils or split peas. Glue the lid firmly into place. Use cord to thread on beads to make the maraca rattle outside as well as inside.

BATHROOM ITEMS

Although very practical, bathroom items can be very dull so cheer them up with one or two flourishes. Paint the child's name on the handle of a new toothbrush, comb or hairbrush with brightly coloured nail varnish. Turn a face flannel into a purse and pack an animal soap into it. Use foam scraps to cut into animal bath sponges.

CLOTHES

Make or buy a pair of woollen mittens. Embroider a woollen face on each woollen mitten and turn them into mittens which will double as glove

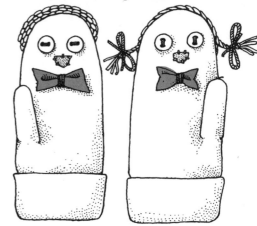

puppets. It would be fun to make one face happy and the other sad, or make one mitten into a boy's face and the other into a girl's face.

A very ordinary pair of slippers can be brought to life by sewing on two bells from the pet shop. Add some fur fabric ears and turn the slippers into two furry animals.

T-shirts with a picture or a message make good presents. Drawn or embroidered names are always popular.

Apart from basic items of clothing there are bow ties, muffs, flannel waistcoats, socks of garish stripes and fantastic frilly petticoats, none of which children need but all are fun to wear.

QUICK AND EASY STOCKING FILLERS

Take an odd sock and turn it into a glove puppet. Take an old wallpaper book and turn it into a collage set. Take a tiny piece of velvet and turn it into a purse, a pincushion or a cushion for the doll's house. Take a broken necklace and turn it into a necklace for a child. Make a fairy wand from a piece of silver-painted dowel rod and a silver paper lace doily or a star cut from cardboard and painted. Stick on a paper plate a candy breakfast bought

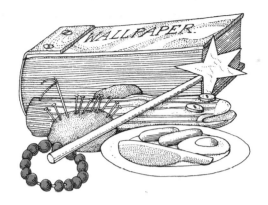

from a rock shop. You can include a sausage, a fried egg, a piece of bacon and half a tomato and call it a breakfast from Father Christmas.

SWEETS

These are often used as stocking fillers. A quick and easy thing to do is to buy the best quality sweets and use just a few of them to make novelties for the stocking. Or try some of the following ideas:

Cover a strip of card with silver foil. Paste on the sweet paper cups as tiny cradles. Cover each jelly baby with a piece of tissue. Add a twisted foil handle for each sweet paper. Individual cradles and babies could hang on the Christmas tree when children are not receiving them in their stockings.

Mix a thin paste of icing sugar. Dab the icing on a card to spell the child's name or to make a picture. Stick on chocolate buttons or use chocolate beans,

peppermints or dolly mixtures. These cards can be hung on the Christmas tree by threading a ribbon through the top of the card and covering with seal-wrap plastic.

Marzipan wraps Grandma and her brothers and sisters always found a packet of marzipan wraps in their Christmas stockings. Individually wrapped in a coat of marzipan were: a cherry; a slice of orange; a brazil, a hazlenut and half a walnut; a piece of chocolate; a raisin, a currant, a date, a sultana and a prune. The children sat on the floor breaking the marzipan treasures open. They kept the things they liked and swapped the things they didn't like. Grandma said that everyone always kept their piece of chocolate but the prune couldn't be given away!

8 oz. (2 cups) ground almonds
4 oz. (½ cup) caster (fine) sugar
4 oz. (½ cup) icing (confectioner's) sugar
few drops of almond essence
approx. 1½—2 eggs

Mix all the dry ingredients together. Add enough egg yolk for a firm mixture; colour if wished. Knead thoroughly, do not over-handle. Roll on a sugared board, cut into fancy shapes and leave exposed to the air to dry.

Fondant

½ lb. icing (confectioner's) sugar
pinch of cream of tartar
1 tbsp evaporated milk
white of an egg

Pound the ingredients together with a wooden spoon in a bowl. Sprinkle a board with sugar and model the fondant by hand. Knead in any of the following flavours: lime, lemon, peppermint, orange, coffee, violet using vegetable colouring to suit the flavour.

Sugar mice and pigs The harvest mouse was an

important character when homes were filled with winter stores. It often appears on Christmas cards – but now remembered affectionately.

Using the fondant mixture, mould a mouse shape fixing a long string tail. Add silver dragées for the eyes, sliced almonds for the ears and fine strips of angelica for the whiskers. Allow to set and wrap in seal wrap.

A plump pink pig makes a good symbolic Christmas gift. Mould the pig by hand, making the legs very firm. A curl of silver foil can be used for the tail. Use silver dragées for the eyes and keep in seal wrap.

Peppermint creams Melt good-quality plain chocolate in a basin over hot water. Roll the peppermint-flavoured fondant into small balls and flatten them. Hold each cream on a large needle and dip into the chocolate. To make the chocolate coating luxuriously thick, dip each cream twice.

Violet or coffee creams Make creams in the same way as peppermint creams, flavouring with violet or coffee essence instead of peppermint, and colour with a few drops of vegetable colouring. Pattern the tips of the creams using the prongs of a fork. Decorate the centre of each cream with crystallized violet or silver dragée.

MAKING GIFTS

Handmade gifts show that care and thought has been taken, and they're more special for giver and receiver. Perhaps it's even more important that no two gifts will be exactly the same. Handmade needn't mean humble either.

We all throw away the best materials for making wrapping paper, gifts, decorations and novelties. It's frustrating to toss a slightly crumpled piece of gold paper into the dustbin only to discover that you could have used it up later for something. Don't throw anything away until you've assessed whether it will be useful. Shopping varies from person to person, and every junk box contains different useful materials. Keep a cardboard box handy to store the various bits and pieces.

WAYS TO ECONOMIZE

Gold and silver paint sprays are quick and easy but potentially dangerous for children to use. They are also very expensive. Instead, buy a small tin of gold or silver paint. It will last longer, spread further and will be more satisfying for children to use.

Buy the narrowest reel of sticky tape. Show children how to use it sparingly. Cut a tiny piece from the reel and stick two pieces of paper together just to show how little is needed.

Mix a pot of wallpaper paste and keep it throughout preparation time. One teaspoonful will thicken and need thinning down every time the paste is used. It will last a long time.

When paste and sticky tape run out, mix a teaspoonful of flour to a thin consistency with water.

Scraps of coloured wool are quite suitable for tying parcels.

Gifts which children can make for adults aren't easy to devise. Young children are anxious to give presentable gifts which have a professional-looking finish to them. Keep any handicraft really simple for the best results.

One year a little girl solved her problem early in the autumn. She filled a large flower pot with garden soil and pressed in some half-rooted strands of honeysuckle. By Christmas the pot was billowing with rooted honeysuckle. It made the perfect gift to offer her grandfather to plant beside his garden shed. He admired her forethought as well as the gift.

If children can manage very little in the way of handwork then the last resort is a calendar which is cheap, simple and always useful.

A NOTEPAD

Cover two squares of card with sticky-backed plastic. Find an interesting picture for the cover. Glue it on. Cut out several squares of paper to fill the notepad. Punch with holes and tie with a ribbon.

A BUTTON BOOK

Cut out two or more sheets of felt and sew them into a book. Use plenty of tiny buttons to make the title. Write 'BUTTON BOOK' before sewing on the buttons of course. Show children how to finish each button firmly on the back.

Sew spare buttons inside the book. Make them into flowers, animals or patterns. The Christmas tree illustrated is easy to copy and would add topicality to the gift.

SNOW SCENE IN A BOTTLE

Find a strong, squat, wide-necked bottle. Plan a scene using small plastic animals or tiny plaster-of-Paris cake decorations. Make sure the models will fit through the neck of the bottle. Brighten the models with coloured nail varnish if necessary. Allow them to dry.

Cover the inside base of the bottle with strong

glue. Glue the bases of the models. Set the models into place using eyebrow tweezers. Leave to dry for twenty-four hours.

Fill the bottle with white vinegar and about two teaspoons of desiccated coconut. Glue the top of the bottle and screw the lid on firmly. Shake to make a snow scene.

MODELLING MATERIALS

Modelling has always been a fascinating occupation for children. Sterile dough makes an excellent substitute for clay or plasticine. Home-made dough costs pence instead of pounds. We once kept some modelling dough in an airtight tin for six months, which was certainly worth its weight in gold for the play value the child had from it.

Basic recipe   Mix together a pound of flour and half a pound of salt. Add just enough water to make a pliable dough. Place the mixture in an airtight container and gift wrap.

To add a little extra stimulus, divide the dough into sections and add a few drops of vegetable colouring to each section, and leave one natural.

For children who are careful about always working with their dough on the kitchen table, a table-spoon of lanolin will make the dough more pliable, but lanolin should be avoided for very young children who drop bits and pieces on the carpet.

PRESENTS FROM FELT

Felt is a time-honoured material to use for gift making. The colours are gloriously vivid, the ends never fray and it's a quick, cheap, cheerful material to use.

There are plenty of patterns in the needlework shops for making felt animals. The following ideas are quick and simple to make as well. Once you've discovered how easy it is to work with felt you will be able to find countless ways of using the basic material.

A tree Cut out a circle of firm card by drawing round a plate and cut in half. Cut out two slightly larger circles of felt and cut in half. Glue a half circle of card into a cone. Cover it with a felt half-circle. Leave to dry. Taking the second circle,

cut into it about 2″ and continue round the outside. Cut two more 'trims' and fringe the edges. Glue the three sets of trim around the tree. Use tiny scraps of felt for making the cut-outs for the decorations. Make robins, stars, bells, crescent moons, angels, flowers and parcels.

A Father Christmas Cut out a circle of firm card and a circle of scarlet felt. Cut a line into the centre of the circle of card and turn it into a cone. Cover the card with the felt. Cut out from scraps a face, arms, cape and a sack which can be given separately for the child to press on, as felt sticks to itself. Cut out gifts and toys to glue at the top of the sack. Glue on to the face two eyes and a mouth, and use white cotton wool for the beard.

A little house Cover a firm cardboard box in felt.

Cut out windows, doors, trees, bikes, trikes, dust-bins, flowers and people. The felt accessories can be arranged on the walls of the house: pack them loose for the child to apply.

DOLLS

A felt family For a toddler make a whole family of little felt dolls. Begin by making a bag with plenty of pockets for 'housing' the dolls. It's exciting to find hidden pockets inside the bag as well as outside.

Cut out plenty of pieces of pink or brown felt, four inches by three inches. Sew up the little bodies. Stuff them with old tights, which have been chopped up, or with cotton wool. Tighten the necks using running stitch, pulling slightly. Use scraps of fabric to make features and clothes. Embroider or sew on the faces.

A giant doll Tiny children love to lug around a companion which is nearly as big as they are. A doll which is almost life-size can be a substitute companion for a toddler who often plays alone. Cut out two doll shapes of the same size out of white or pink sailcloth, linen, or cotton. Sew the pieces together and stuff with Kapok. Use odd wool for the hair and buttons for the eyes. Embroider on the features. Use outworn children's clothes for dressing the doll.

A patchwork doll This is fun to make and demands little sewing skill. Collect together plenty of cotton fabric scraps in bright colours, a length of cord, a bell, and needles and cotton.

Cut out plenty of circles by drawing round a cup. Sew with a running stitch round each circle and draw it up. Draw round a teaplate to make the

head. Embroider a cheerful face. Stuff the head with an old pair of nylon tights.

Sew the cord firmly onto the base of the head. Flatten the circles and thread them on. Add a circle to the top of the head for a hat. Sew the bell firmly on the hat.

Tie a loop of cord to the base of the body to thread on the circles for the legs. Tie a length of cord to the body to tie on the arms.

POP-UP PUPPET

Little children love these, and they are fun and easy to make.

Cut a large circle out of stiff card by drawing around a dinner plate. Cut the circle in half and bend it round to make a cone (leave a hole at the top), and fix with non-toxic glue.

For the head, draw around a large breakfast cup on to plain fabric and cut out. Gather around the circle, stuff with cotton wool or chopped-up tights, and glue it on one end of a dowel rod.

Cut out a circle of fabric slightly bigger than the base cone for the body. Cut a hole in the centre and gather into the neck, sewing it to the base of the head.

Cut out a semi-circle of fabric which is slightly larger than the base, and glue it on the base, turning in the margins top and bottom. Invert the cone and slip the rod down into it. Pleat and glue the hem of the body around the top of the cone.

Add a cheerful face and two long arms using scraps of felt. Buttons will make bright eyes providing they are well sewn on.

62

PLANTS

Flower pots can be decorated by covering a pot with plastic wood filler. Cover the pot liberally. While it is still damp press in shells, pebbles or pieces of coloured broken glass.

Babies Tears (or Mind Your Own Business) This pretty plant spills out all over the pot until a dainty mound of green leaves is formed. It's an easy plant to keep indoors or out. Babies Tears would make an ideal gift for the parents of a young baby.

Herbs A pot of fresh herbs would make a delightful gift. Perennial herbs are the most useful and can be grown in a pot from cuttings taken in the summer. Easy favourites to grow are Winter Savory, Silver Embroidered Thyme or Golden Thyme.

Buy a pâté dish from the delicatessen—these are usually sold off cheaply. Drill three holes in the base for drainage. Line the base with pebbles or broken crocks and fill with good compost. Settle plants into the bowl during the late summer while they are still growing vigorously. Pinch off the top shoots to make them bush out. Keep them on a sunny windowsill and don't overwater them once they're established.

Bi-coloured hyacinth Buy a blue and a pink hyacinth bulb. Slice both bulbs with a really sharp knife through the centre. Press half a pink and half a blue hyacinth bulb together. Seal the sides with sticky tape. Plant the bulb in a pot using good bulb fibre. Keep the bulb damp and in a warm place until the leaves appear. Present the plant with just the spikes of the leaves showing. Retard the growth if necessary. In just a few weeks the recipient will be amazed to find a pink and blue hyacinth flower.

A beautiful picture is simple to make using garden flowers. Since pressed flowers are very delicate they will need a delicate fabric for the background. Using plain pale silky fabric, cover a board. Find a picture frame to size. Spend some time working on the arrangement before gluing permanently into position. Use the glue sparingly. Slip the board inside the frame. To make smaller pictures, buy a photograph frame.

PRESSED FLOWERS AND LEAVES

While walking through the woods or parkland, keep an eye open for tiny wild flowers, seeded grass heads, coloured autumn leaves and ferns. Press them between the leaves of an old book inside sheets of tissue. In a few weeks they will be ready for use. Garden flowers can be gathered in the summer and pressed as well. They may take longer to press than wild flowers, especially if they have fleshy leaves, stalks and petals.

HERBAL CUSHIONS

Dry some herbs by picking bunches of them in the early autumn and hanging them in a warm shady place. When they are completely dry, crush them coarsely and fill a small cotton or muslin bag. Basil, camomile, hops and scented geranium leaves are suitable for a herbal cushion. Avoid the stimulating herbs which go into a potpourri such as thyme, hyssop, lavender and mint.

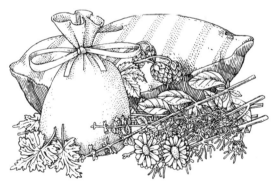

LAVENDER

Lavender was used strewn among the rushes on the floor and placed in the linen chest to keep out the moths. It was also used for making potpourri, perfumed soaps, bath oil and even perfumed icing.

Although traditionally called a lavender 'bottle',
the name is derived from its shape as no glass is involved. To make one, pick twenty-four heads of long-stemmed lavender when the weather is dry and the lavender is almost in full bloom. Tie the heads tightly using a long piece of lavender-coloured baby ribbon. Leave a shorter end for tying a bow. Bend the stalks up over the flower heads. Weave the ribbon through the stalks in pairs. Tie tightly to finish and make a bow. Trim the stalks.

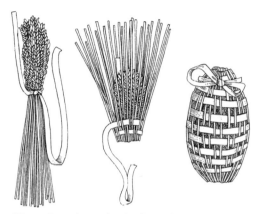

To make a lavender bath, pick a large bunch of English lavender in the autumn when it's in full bloom. Dry it and then shred the flowerheads from the stalks. Draw round a small cup to make circles out of fine material such as nylon net or muslin. Fill each circle of fabric with the flowerheads. Tie tightly with pink, blue, white or lavender baby ribbon. Pack the bags into a box covered with seal wrap with the instructions: 'LAVENDER BATH. PLACE ONE IN A BATH AND LEAVE IT THERE.'

For lavender bags, cut out larger circles and fill as with the lavender bath. Tie tightly with a ribbon, leaving a loop for hanging the bag on to a coat hanger.

To make lavender bag crackers, use strips of fabric rather than circles. Pack the shredded lavender into the fabric. Roll it up. Tie both ends with a ribbon. Fringe or scallop the edges.

The Druids lit bonfires all over the land on the darkest, longest night of the year. The fires were an encouragement to the mighty sun god, to re-awaken with his essential power of heat and light. The Norsemen filled their homes with lighted candles. They held a long festival of candlelight during the darkest days of winter. Like the Druids, the aim was to cheer the winter gloom and at the same time to honour the sun. A carol service held in candlelight has a very special atmosphere.

Today, Italian children sing 'Santa Lucia'; the Scandinavian children perform the Lucia Celebration, wearing a crown of spruce and four lighted candles; both take place at the time of the shortest day of the year on or near 12/13 of December.

CANDLEMAKING

The most mess and the most fun we have ever had in our kitchen came from candlemaking. As craft work it really is most suitable for teenagers who know the rules for handling hot fats. For younger children, it is quite safe to use slightly cooled wax providing an adult is at hand to assist. The glory of it is that the failures can be remoulded or disguised and used in other ways. Scraps of candles can be used up as well.

Basic equipment Candles can be made using very little basic equipment. To begin, buy a bag of paraffin wax, granules or powder, a card of medium wick and a small packet of stearin from a craft or art shop. Find a sharp knife, an old saucepan and some empty plastic or paper containers like yoghurt pots to use as moulds. The moulds should be slightly wider at the top or the candles would be difficult to remove. Melt some wax with ten per cent of stearin: it can be measured with a tablespoon. Fix a length of wick to the base of the container with either a tiny blob of melted wax or a tiny piece of plasticine. Suspend the wick by

winding it around an old pencil laid across the top of the container. Heat the wax slowly. Have a saucepan lid ready to extinguish flames in case any hot wax spills on to the cooker. If water is thrown on to burning wax it will react in the same way as hot fat by flaring up. When a candle is set a dip may appear around the wick. Add a little more melted wax. Always pour the melted wax into the centre of the mould. Avoid pouring wax against the edge of the mould or it makes bubbles which will spoil the finished work. The following four suggestions are reasonably safe for young children to make.

A MARBLED CANDLE

Use a plain domestic candle.

You will need: some ordinary domestic candles, an old scrap of red wax crayon or the remains of a red lipstick, and an old saucepan. Boil some water. Melt the wax or lipstick on the water. It will form into runny blobs. Cool it slightly. Let the child hold the candle by the wick and swirl it around in the hot water. Remove it, and then hold the other end of the candle and dip the top. The candle will set at once with a marbled effect.

CRUSHED WAX CANDLE

Buy a packet of paraffin wax, a small packet of stearin and a card of medium-sized wick. (Use up

old scraps of candles which are too short to burn. Grate them and add them to the mixture.)

Prepare a yoghurt pot mould by burning a hole in the base with a hot needle. Thread the wick through the hole, knot it and firm it into place with a blob of plasticine. Tie the top of the wick to a pencil and suspend it across the top of the pot. Melt some of the wax over a low heat. Add a little grated coloured wax crayon. As soon as the wax is melted whip it in a basin with a fork. While it is still warm press the coloured wax into the base of the pot around the wick. Keep repeating until the pot is full of coloured layers. Remove the candle from the pot. Cut the wick to the right length. Some of these will be suitable for children to give as gifts.

A coloured layered candle made from crushed wax can look very effective made in a glass. Fix the wick to the base of the glass with a small blob of plasticine or melted wax.

SNOWBALLS

Cut down a candle or use an old candle which has burned down. Fix about a third of a domestic candle onto a dish with a drop of melted wax. Melt some wax and a little stearin in a pan over a low heat. Pour the melted wax into a small basin and whip it with a fork. Before the wax cools press it round the candle stump to make a snowball.

A SNOWMAN

Use a full-length domestic candle to make this. Melt the wax in the same way as for snowballs. Whip it in a basin and mould it into a snowball on the lower two-thirds of the candle. As soon as it's set, mould on the head using more whipped wax to cover the top of the candle. Leave the wick showing. Scraps of paper, paint or wax crayons can be used to make the features and clothes of the snowman.

A NIGHT LIGHT

This recipe comes from a book entitled *The School of Arts*, published in 1754.

To make a continual light by night, (into a bottle put) an ounce of the oil of almonds, half a drachm of phosphorous and two or three grains of flour of sulphur into it. Hold it in a gentle warmth to dissolve, then shake the bottle and draw your cork and you will have a fine glow-worm light. If you rub a little on the rim or any other part, it will appear all in flame.

You should be able to obtain the necessary ingredients from any chemist's. Just to modernize the 'glow-worm' slightly, and to make it into a highly acceptable and intriguing gift, mix a few drops of pine essence into the almond oil. Present it in an elegant vinegar bottle. Don't forget to attach the instructions for lighting it.

A MAGIC BREW

Melt enough wax to fill a green-stemmed glass. Dip the wick and fix to the base of the glass with a few drops of melted wax. Colour the wax red and leave off the heat for a few moments. Fill the glass nearly to the rim. Melt some white wax and whip it as it cools. Set this on top of the red wax so that it billows over the rim. As the white wax sets, sprinkle on some glitter.

A PINT OF FOAMING ALE

Melt enough brown wax to fill a pint tumbler. Dip the wick and fix to the base of the tumbler. Pour in the brown wax. Whip enough white wax to make a foaming head.

WALNUT SHELL BOATS

Fill halves of walnut shells with melted wax and give each one a tiny wick. These look very pretty floating on a dish of water.

CHRISTMAS TREE

This is made using a green domestic candle as a base. Hold the candle over melted green wax and drip it on to the candle using a wooden spoon. Begin at the base to increase the girth of the candle and slowly work up to the top. When the green tree is set, add snow by dripping on clear white wax.

ROSES

These are moulded by hand from various colours of wax. As the melted wax cools, pour a small amount over a wooden spoon. Peel the wax off the spoon and form into petal shape. The petals can be attached by using extra wax which is still hot.

GIFT WRAPPING

WRAPPING PAPER

Paper is expensive, and paper torn eagerly is wasteful and can be messy. But half the fun of Christmas gifts is in trying to guess what's inside and in unwrapping crinkly crunchy parcels. Also, attractively wrapped gifts arranged around the Christmas tree can add to the decorations.

Crêpe paper is good value compared with other wrappings. Buy a packet of crêpe paper in bright holly red or mistletoe green. Wrap parcels in the solid colour and dress them with contrasting ribbon and bows. You can also chop the crêpe into thick strips to use as ribbons. Wrap the parcels with plain white lining paper and tie them lavishly with crêpe paper bows.

CHILDREN'S PAPER

It can be fun for children to help decorate a roll of wallpaper lining to use as their own wrapping paper. Unroll a length of lining paper on to the kitchen table. Cover the paper with any of the following suggestions until children tire and need to make a change of pattern. Just keep changing patterns until the whole roll has been decorated.

Mix a thick pot of poster or powder paint in a bright Christmas colour. Add a tiny pinch of wallpaper paste to make the mixture really thick. Pour some paint into an old saucer lined with a thickly folded paper towel. Cut a potato in half. Carve out a design. Begin printing by dabbing the potato into the saucer then on to the lining paper. (A really good print on a potato can be used for making Christmas cards as well.)

Gather a handful of real holly leaves or ferns. Make a thick mixture of paint, adding a pinch of wallpaper paste. Place a holly leaf or fern down on the paper. Dab round the edges to stencil the shape.

Cut out stars, leaves, crescent moons or Christmas trees. Place them down on the lining paper and use them in the same way as the natural stencils.

Place real ferns or holly leaves on the lining paper. Splash over them using thin paint. Flick the end of a stencil brush or an old toothbrush with the thumb.

Find an old pencil which has a rubber on the end. Mix a little thick red poster paint. Use the rubber end of the pencil as a print. Lavishly cover the paper with red holly berries.

GIFT BOXES

One small pot of gold or silver paint will cover several cardboard boxes and plastic containers. An hour spent doing this one evening will ensure that there are plenty of Christmas containers ready to be used when it's time to wrap the gifts.

To cover a box with Christmas wrapping paper, paste the base of the box. Press on the wrapping paper by pressing out creases and air bubbles from the centre. Paste the sides one at a time, and press out any air bubbles. Cover the lid by beginning in the centre. Press firmly and then complete by pasting the sides. Mitre the corners as the work progresses.

CORDS

Cords are so easy to make that I couldn't believe my eyes the first time I saw two men making a temporary rope. They simply took some straw, then they gently twisted it into a length and gradually pulled harder and harder, twisting in opposite directions.

Take six wool threads of the same length. Tie each end to a pencil. Two people pull the threads and twist in opposite directions. When the cord begins to double twist in the centre, halve it and repeat the operation. Any number of threads can be used according to the thickness required. Cords are useful for tying gifts, suspending decorations or for macramé work.

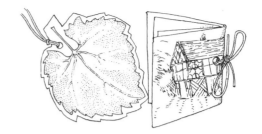

GIFT TAGS

Use one well-formed autumn leaf to make a gift tag. Coat the leaf with colourless nail varnish. Paste it on to a small card. Punch a hole and attach a short length of ribbon for looping the tag on to a parcel.

Fans always formed part of the Victorian decorations. Make some gift tag fans by pleating Christmas paper and pasting them on to card. Write the message on the back.

Decorate your packages with bright ribbons and bows. For an elegant finish, tie on a cluster of fir cones or beechnut husks. Or, for a child's package, make a bow and then tie into the bow peppermint rock and other sweets.

To make a bow: use self-adhesive Christmas ribbon.

Make a spring bow by making circles out of the ribbon, starting off with a small circle and increasing the size of the circle each time you go round. Tape the base on to the package.

Drum Paint an economy-sized coffee tin with silver paint. Make some long red- and white-striped cords from wool. Glue a thick strip of card round the base and the top of the tin. Glue on the cords.

Bauble Wrap a small gift in tissue. Draw around a plate and cut out a circle of crêpe paper and a circle of cellophane. Serrate the edges. Place the gift in the centre of both rings and fix at the top with sticky tape.

A Christmas tree Cut out a semi-circle of card by drawing around a dinner plate. Glue into shape. Cut out a long strip of green fringed paper and paste on. Paste on a circular base.

You can also use the same basic method to make tall cones to turn them into witches', dunces' or clowns' hats.

NOVELTY PACKAGES

These can be used to wrap awkwardly shaped presents as well as to disguise obvious shapes and create a bit of fun.

Dice Turn a square box into a dashing dice. Cover a box with plain bright paper, making neatly folded corners. Cut out some bold dots from plain contrasting paper. Make a matching gift tag by folding a card covered with the same paper, dotted on the outside and the message written on the inside.

Suitcase Turn a shirt box into a suitcase. Cover by pasting with brown paper. Draw on hinges and straps with a black felt tip pen. Make a card handle

and paste on to the top of the package. Cut out circles of Christmas paper and stick inside each a small circle of white paper. Print London, Paris, Rome, New York in the centres. Use a luggage label for the gift tag.

Candle Turn a tall cylinder into a candle. Stick a spiral of coloured paper from the base to the top. Cut out a card to make the flame and wick. Colour the flame yellow, orange and red.

Elf Wrap a cylinder with a bright, plain paper. Concertina arms and legs for the elf from card. Make a pointed hat and funny face from felt or coloured gum paper.

PART IV

THE FEAST

Now thrice welcome Christmas,
  Which brings us good cheer,
Minced pies and plum porridge,
  Good ale and strong beer;

With pig, goose and capon,
  The best that may be,
So well doth the weather
  And our stomachs agree.

FOOD

Traditionally the 'Good Wife' began preparing for Christmas as the harvest was gathered. Before the days of fridges and freezers planning ahead was not just an economic necessity: pickling, drying, storing and preserving food and herbs meant survival for the family when little fresh food could be grown. The housewife knew that there would be hard times ahead through the cold winter months. The annual food supply varied between the plenty of harvest and the leanness of Lent.

Bunches of dried herbs gained increasingly in importance as the quality of the meat deteriorated. Warm spices were imported, which not only gave a pleasantly comforting flavour, but which hid the fact that some meat was 'On the turn'.

'Nose, nose, jolly red nose,
And what gave thee this jolly red nose?'
'Nutmeg, ginger, cinnamon and cloves,
That's what gave me this jolly red nose!'

'Nutmeg, ginger, cinnamon and cloves', the spices mentioned in the old rhyme, give a rosy glow when their names are chanted. They sound warm and they taste warming. Christmas was the great time for making sweetmeats. Many of them are really simple to produce. All that is needed is a little planning in the weeks leading up to Christmas. It would certainly add someting to a traditional Christmas if the mincemeat was homemade, and stuffing is almost as simple to make as to buy.

Thomas Tusser was a great Elizabethan recorder of everyday things. He tells us:

At Hallowtide slaughter time entereth in
And then doth the husbandman's feasting begin;
From thence until Shrovetide kill now and then some,
Their offal for household the better will come.

And of Christmas cheer he says:

Beef, mutton and pork, shred pies of the best,
Pig, veal, goose and capon, and turkey well drest;
Cheese, apples and nuts, jolly carols to hear,
As then in the country is counted good cheer.

It's little wonder that the Italians of the Elizabethan court reported home that nothing was so busy as an English oven at Christmas. The Italians now use this as a saying about anyone who is really busy: 'He's as busy as an English oven at Christmas.'

The further back we search for information the busier the Christmas cooking seems to have been. In 1206, King John commanded the Sheriff of Hampshire to procure 1500 chickens, 5000 eggs, 20 oxen, 100 pigs and 100 sheep. Christmas was a time for 'large tabling and belly cheer'. Obviously the court didn't intend to go short as they celebrated the season in Winchester Castle.

THE TURKEY

The plump stuffed bird which forms the main meat dish of our table today bears little resemblance to the scrawny birds which were snared by the poorer settlers in Virginia. Wealthy colonial settlers could lavish their families with venison, ham and beef and despised the humble turkey.

At the turn of the twentieth century the turkey was on its way by boat to the British Isles, along with that staple vegetable, the potato.

HOW TO PREPARE A TURKEY

More of us get into difficulty cooking the Christmas turkey than with any other kitchen task we undertake. A hundred years ago women cooked enormous joints of meat with complete confidence. Today the turkey is usually the largest piece of meat any of us ever cook.

A large frozen turkey will take about three days to thaw completely. Prepare the bird on Christmas Eve to avoid panic because it can be time-consuming. Remove the giblets and wash the bird thorough-

ly inside and out. Stuff the body with chestnut stuffing and stuff the crop with sausage meat. Rub the skin of the bird with half a lemon and dash with salt and pepper. Cover with aluminium foil and surround with small rolls of streaky bacon and chipolatas. Allow 30 minutes per pound plus 30 minutes over, up to 12 lb.; allow only 12 minutes over for heavier birds. Cook at 350°F, gas mark 4. Cook the roast potatoes in the same roasting tin if there is enough space. Baste the turkey occasionally while roasting. Raw turkey is revolting. If the carcass doesn't seem to be cooking right through, cut off the legs and cook them in a separate dish.

CARVING THE TURKEY

Grand families carve the turkey in the dining room. Learner carvers might prefer the following method. The carver should have ready plenty of hot plates, a heated meat dish, and carving knife and fork. Let the turkey stand for 10 minutes or so: it will firm up, making it easier to carve.

Begin by cutting the legs off the bird. Carve some of the brown meat off the legs and return it to the warm oven. Try to imagine that the carcass of the bird is a box, and slice straight down the side, taking off a thin slice of breast.

The Parson's nose The carver is allowed to have some fun after carving the turkey. Put the Parson's nose on to the plate of the child who will complain loudest. Don't forget to mention that the Parson's nose is a great delicacy. If the children are all on the lookout for the Parson's nose, hide it on the victim's plate under a piece of meat!

The wishbone Whoever finds the wishbone on their Christmas plate is lucky. However, to win the chance of making a wish the winner of the wishbone must pull it with a partner. Whoever wins the longest bone, as it snaps, wins a wish. The winner must close his eyes tightly and wish hard, and not tell anyone the wish or it's bad luck.

BREAD SAUCE

Peel an onion, keeping it whole. Spike it with a few cloves. Simmer the onion in half a pint of milk with a bay leaf until the milk is well flavoured and the onion is soft. Season to taste. Add two small handfuls of soft white breadcrumbs. Continue cooking over a low heat for about 15 minutes and then remove onion and bay leaf. Add a knob of butter and a little grated nutmeg.

Bread sauce can be made before Christmas Day and re-heated over a low heat. (Serves 6-8).

CHESTNUT STUFFING

You will need about 2 lb. of chestnuts for a small 10 lb. turkey. Split the tops of the chestnuts with a sharp knife. Place them in boiling water for 30 minutes. Add a little salt. Drain and remove the tough outer and inner skins. If the skins are difficult to remove stand them again in boiling water for a few minutes.

Reheat the chestnuts in a little butter with a dash of salt and pepper. They are cooked when they begin to pulp.

Sieve or chop nuts finely. Heat 4 oz. ($\frac{1}{4}$ cup) butter or fat and add 2 large chopped onions and 8 oz. (1 cup) chopped celery. When the onion and the celery are cooked, add to the chestnuts with 4 oz. (1 cup) chopped bacon and 4 oz. (1 cup) breadcrumbs. Season with salt, pepper and thyme to taste.

THE NOTTINGHAM GOOSE FAIR

Christmas is coming, the geese are getting fat,
Please put a penny in the old man's hat.
If you haven't got a penny, a ha'penny will do.
If you haven't got a ha'penny, then God bless you!

The City of Nottingham was granted a charter in 1284 to hold a goose fair. The Michaelmas fair is

still held today. In olden days people would travel from near and far to make the selection of a live goose for their Christmas table. The bird was taken home and fattened on the finest grain. When we use the common expression, 'She's really

cooked her goose!' we can understand how vital it was to make the winter stores last out.

ROAST GOOSE

| 1 goose | fat for basting |
| sage and onion stuffing | flour |

To prepare the goose for the oven, make the stuffing and insert this into the body. Truss the goose and prick the skin of the breast. Roast the bird in a fairly hot oven, 375-400°F, gas mark 5-6; calculate 25-30 minutes per pound, plus 30 minutes. When almost cooked, dredge the breast with flour, baste with some hot fat and leave to brown. Remove trussing and dish up the bird.

Serve with apple sauce and beef gravy; goose gravy made from simmered giblets can be served instead.

BAKED HAM

A large ham, baked in the old way using the method housewives employed when bread was baked in a brick oven, is really delicious. Served as cold slices it is also a useful joint when entertaining or for snacks.

1 ham   brown sugar
flour   cloves

Soak the ham in water for at least 12 hours. Wipe well and trim off any rusty bits. Coat with a flour and water dough which must be sufficiently thick to keep in all the juices. Place in a fairly hot oven (400°F, gas mark 6) for about 15 minutes, then reduce the heat to cool (310°F, gas mark 2) and cook allowing 30 minutes per lb.

Remove the dough crust and skin. Score squares in the fat and place a clove in each square, sprinkle brown sugar over the fat. Garnish the knuckle with a paper frill.

Our good Quane Bess she maayde a pudden,
An' stuffed 'un vull o' plums.
An' in it she put gurt dabs o' vat,
As big as my two thumbs.

GIBLET PIE

No part of the bird was wasted. The feathers would be used for stuffing a cushion or pillow, and the giblets went into a tasty pie.

goose giblet   puff pastry (6 oz./1½ cups
1 lb. of rump steak   of flour, 3 oz./⅓ cup
1 sliced onion   of fat)
milk for glazing   bouquet garni
    salt and pepper

Wash giblets. Put in a pan with sliced onion, bouquet garni and seasoning to taste. Cover with cold water, and simmer for about two hours.

Slice the steak thinly and season it. Place alternate layers of steak and giblets in a pie dish. Strain over enough stock from the pan to come three-quarters of the way up the dish. Allow meat to cool and cover with pastry. Bake in a hot oven, 425-450°F, gas mark 7-8, until pastry is set. Reduce heat and continue cooking until meat is tender: for about an hour at 350°F, gas mark 4.

Glaze with milk 20 minutes before the pie is served.

"WE ALL WANT SOME FIGGY PUDDING"

In winter, when there was no fresh fruit, the dried figs, currants, sultanas, raisins, prunes and nuts which housewives stored were an essential part of the diet. Flour was coarse and brown. The Christmas pudding went through several stages before it evolved as the steamed pudding we enjoy today. It began as figgy porridge and then plum porridge superseded it. Plum pudding came next and was boiled in a bag. Perhaps this is why Christmas card artists persist in depicting the pudding as a complete circle. Today we eat a tall, steamed pudding. It is cooked thoroughly before Christmas Day. On Christmas morning, one of the first chores is to

put the pudding on to steam. Unless it is heated right through it may not blaze up when the brandy is poured over it.

The blazing Christmas pudding has absolutely nothing to do with the Nativity. It is quite simply a Druid ritual. When the pudding is carried into the dining room the family is performing a sun-worshipping ceremony. The high priestess, who cooked the pudding and set it alight, is reassuring her congregation that the sun will shine again soon.

It is lucky to deck the pudding with a sprig of holly. The holly is a symbol of everlasting life.

Long ago it became the tradition to make the puddings one year and to serve them the next. Some households still do this. Of course, a pudding containing plenty of spirits will keep for a long time. Many families follow the practice of making the puddings on 'Stir-up Sunday' which is the last Sunday after Trinity and the week before the first Sunday in Advent. The custom has a practical side—preparing the pudding in plenty of time—but the name comes from the Collect for the day: 'Stir up, we beseech thee, O Lord, the wills of Thy faithful people.'

Of course, everyone who stirs the pudding three times can make a wish. A clever woman must have invented this idea, because stirring the sticky ingredients takes a good deal of elbow grease, so if every member of the family stirred the pudding and made a wish the work was soon finished. It was good luck, too, if every member of the family stirred the pudding because it meant that everyone was safely home.

LUCKY CHARMS AND SILVER JOEYS

In Tudor times the lucky reveller who found the ring or coin hidden in the cake wore a paper crown and became the Lord of Misrule. However lowly his station, the Lord of Misrule could order his superiors about and confer forfeits upon the assembled throng.

Wealthy Victorians baked their Twelfth-night cake with silver charms inside. Anyone who found a charm in a slice of cake had their fortune told for the coming year. There was always an anchor, a pair of wedding bells, a button and a four-leafed clover. The charms were made of the very thin silver and sold on a card.

During the depression between the two world wars the poor copied this custom, but instead of silver charms inside the Twelfth-night cake they used threepenny joeys inside the Christmas pudding The threepenny joey was a tiny silver coin worth half a sixpence. Today this would be worth 1¼ pence. Sixpences in the pudding have become a modern form of treasure trove.

NANA GRENDER'S CHRISTMAS PUDDING

6 oz. (1 cup) currants	8 oz. (¼ cup) brown sugar
6 oz. (1 cup) sultanas	½ tsp. mixed spice
12 oz. (2 cups) raisins	1 oz. ground almonds
3 oz. (½ cup) mixed peel	grated rind of 1 lemon
4 oz. (1 cup) flour	¼ grated nutmeg
pinch of salt	4 eggs
8 oz. (2 cups) breadcrumbs	3 oz. (⅓ cup) glacé cherries
8 oz. (1 cup) suet	brandy

Wash and pick over the currants and sultanas, stone the raisins and chop the peel. Put all the ingredients into a bowl, mix thoroughly with the beaten eggs and enough brandy (or old ale) to moisten the whole; pour into well-greased moulds and cover with greased paper. Steam for 8 or 9 hours. Tie a string beneath the rim of the pudding basin and across the top. This will make a useful handle and avoid any possible scalds when dishing up. Serve with brandy butter or sauce.

Christmas pudding may be steamed for 6 to 7 hours, allowed to become cold and the steaming time completed when it is to be served. If the paper covering the pudding is changed, the pudding can be stored for several months in a cool, dry place.

To set a pudding alight, make sure the pudding is heated right through. Heat the brandy a little before pouring it over the pudding, and serve it on a heated dish.

BRANDY BUTTER

Beat 4 oz. (½ cup) of butter until it is soft. Add a little caster (fine) sugar until the mixture is stiff. Flavour with a few drops of vanilla essence and a little liqueur brandy.

To make a creamy sauce, whisk ¼ pint double (whipping) cream until thick, then add 1 level tablespoon icing (confectioner's) sugar. Gradually stir in 1 to 2 tablespoons brandy to taste.

Both versions can be made at any time during the week before Christmas. Keep it in an airtight container in the refrigerator until an hour before serving.

GRANDMA PERRY'S SHERRY CAKE

1 lb. (2 cups) mixed fruit
2 oz. ($\frac{1}{4}$ cup) glacé cherries
3 oz. ($\frac{1}{2}$ cup) mixed peel
3 eggs
$\frac{1}{4}$ pint sherry

6 oz. ($\frac{1}{3}$ cup) butter
8 oz. (2 cups) self-raising flour
2 oz. (1 cup) ground almonds
small pinch of salt, cinnamon, nutmeg
grated rind of 1 lemon

Soak chopped cherries, mixed peel and dried fruit in the sherry for at least a week. Stir from time to time. Grease and line a large cake tin. Cream together butter and sugar. Gently stir in the eggs. Add the rest of the ingredients, leaving the flour until last. Cover with foil or greaseproof paper and bake for 1 hour at 350°F, gas mark 4.

Reduce oven heat and bake for 1½ hours more. Cool in the tin, and then turn out on to cake wire. Cool overnight before decorating.

APRICOT GLAZE

Before attempting to cover the Christmas cake with almond paste, brush over a coating of apricot glaze which will help to make it stick firmly. Mix and bring to the boil 2 tablespoons of apricot jam and 1 of water. Brush the mixture over the cake.

ALMOND PASTE

almond essence
2 eggs
$\frac{1}{2}$ lb. ground almonds

$\frac{1}{2}$ lb. (1 cup) caster sugar
1 tsp. orange flower water
half a lemon

Stir the almonds, a few drops of almond essence, sugar and egg yolks in a pan over a gentle heat. Reduce the mixture to paste, add the orange flower water, the juice of the lemon and the beaten white of one egg. If the mixture is too thick to work easily, add a little more lemon juice. This amount will cover a 3 lb. cake.

ICING

white of 2 large eggs
12 oz. (1½ cups) caster (fine) sugar
good pinch of salt

1 tbsp. water
½ tsp. cream of tartar
juice of 1 lemon

Beat the egg whites until thick, then gradually add the other ingredients and whisk together. Put the bowl over a pan of hot water and continue to whisk until the mixture forms peaks. Spread at once, and decorate. Leave in a cool place overnight before serving.

CAKE DECORATIONS

You can make silver leaves by covering holly leaves with silver foil. Use small red sweets or red dragées to make edible berries.

For real leaves, gather a handful of holly and ivy leaves and wash thoroughly. Press them flat for a short time. Line a baking sheet with greaseproof paper and spread out the leaves. Sprinkle them with icing sugar. Melt a bar of chocolate over a basin of hot water. Pour melted chocolate over each leaf. Peel the chocolate leaves from the real leaves very carefully. Store them away until they are needed.

In our house the little snowboys and huge reindeer come out. They have been handed down through several generations, and the children love to scatter them about the cake every year.

AUNT EVE'S STORY

'The highlight of Christmas dinner came at the very end of the meal. By the time we had finished eating night was falling. We turned down the gaslight to darken the room. The youngest children began to look worried. Suddenly Father would come into the dining room carrying aloft a flaming meat dish.

'The dish was piled high with muscatels and raisins. Blue brandy flames licked up from it.

Father placed the dish in the centre of the table with the words, "God bless you all".

'We chanted back, "God Bless the master of this house, likewise the mistress too".

'This was the signal for everyone to plunge their hands into the flaming dish to snatch at the fruit and nuts. By this time the little children screamed their heads off with fright. I still remember it with a shivery thrill. It was a real kerfuffle. Someone always ended up crying with someone else's elbow in their eye. By the time we turned the gaslight back up the dish was quite empty. It was funny really. Father never went into the kitchen. For years I thought he was a magician on Christmas Day.'

BRANDY SNATCH

Heat a large shallow dish. Fill with muscatels and nuts. Pour brandy over the mixture and set alight. The Brandy Snatch was made into a game, and was popular with Victorians. The players must quickly snatch the fruit and nuts from the flames and put them in their mouths.

MINCE PIES

Dame get up and bake your pies,
On Christmas Day, on Christmas Day,
Dame get up and bake your pies,
On Christmas Day in the morning.

Dame what makes your ducks to die?
Ducks to die? Ducks to die?
Dame what makes your ducks to die?
On Christmas Day in the morning.

Their wings are cut, they cannot fly,
Cannot fly, cannot fly.
Their wings are cut they cannot fly,
On Christmas Day in the morning.

In the Victorian days the mince pie was a meal in itself. As the name suggests a mince pie contained minced meat such as ham, tongue, roast beef, or

roast lamb. Spices and a few finely chopped almonds were added. The pastry was baked without a lid and usually in the form of a cradle. It was unlucky to cut a mince pie because the cradle-shaped pie represented the cradle of the Christ Child. A country name for mince pies was 'Mutton Pies'. This suggests that cold roast lamb was the most usual basic meat ingredient.

A delicious way to have mince pies is to serve them piping hot with cream or custard—you could even prise up the lid and insert a dollop of cream just before serving.

Mincemeat 'The ingredients for mincemeat vary considerably, almost every cook having her own recipe,' says the good old *Household Encyclopaedia*.

If children only make homemade mincemeat once in their lives at least they will grow up knowing about the basic ingredients which go into this very traditional pie filling.

Pare, core and finely chop 2 lb. of apples. Add 1 lb. each of currants, stoned and chopped raisins and brown sugar, ½ lb. of very finely chopped suet, ¼ lb. candied peel (chopped very small), a level dessertspoonful of powdered allspice, a pinch of salt and the juice and grated rinds of two lemons. A little brandy or rum may be used to moisten it, and a little raisin or other wine. Mix the ingredients very thoroughly (this is where the children can help), cover with a cloth and let the mincemeat stand for some hours before putting it into small jars with seal wrap or greaseproof paper.

BRANDY SNAPS

Don't serve these on Christmas Day. They can easily be stored in an airtight tin and served in the days after Christmas. They are certainly useful for helping to use up leftover cream, and children will enjoy rolling the shapes around wooden spoon handles as well as helping to fill them with cream later.

2 oz. (¼ cup) butter	1 level tsp. ground ginger
2 oz. (¼ cup) caster (extra-fine) sugar	1 tsp. brandy
	whipped cream
2 oz. (2 tbsp.) golden syrup	
2 oz. (½ cup) plain flour	

Grease the handles of several wooden spoons and two or three flat baking trays.

Slowly heat the butter, sugar and syrup in a saucepan until the butter is melted. Remove from the heat and stir in flour, ginger and brandy. Place teaspoonsful of the mixture well spaced on to the baking trays. Bake for 8 to 10 minutes in a moderate oven 350°F or gas mark 4.

Allow to cool for a minute. Loosen each flat biscuit with a knife and roll them at once round a wooden spoon handle. As soon as the biscuits harden slip them from the spoon with a knife. Fill with whipped cream for serving.

MARZIPAN FRUITS

There can be few gifts of sweets which have a more exotic appearance than a box of marzipan fruits. These are easy to make at home, require very little artistic skill and very little cooking.

Begin by crystallizing plenty of mint leaves in late summer. Pick a generous handful of mint leaves. Wash and dry them. Stir an egg white. Add a little green vegetable colouring if desired. Paint each leaf on both sides with egg white. Then coat them with caster sugar. Spread the leaves out on a sheet of greaseproof paper, and dry them off in a slightly warm oven. Store the crystallized leaves in an airtight tin between sheets of greaseproof paper until they're needed. Crystallized leaves are extremely brittle, so make plenty to allow for some breakages.

Using the basic almond paste mixture (see p. 78) add a few drops of almond essence. Mould the mixture into small apples, pears, cherries, oranges, bananas or apricots. Paint the fruits using a small paint brush and vegetable colouring. Use cloves to make stems and decorate with crystallized mint leaves.

Marzipan can also be used in the same way as fondant for making little novelties for children. Not all children like the taste of marzipan. It's sensible to discover whether children prefer marzipan or fondant before making any novelties for the tree or for stocking fillers. (See page 57 for making fondant novelties for children.)

APPLE RINGS

The best time to make apple rings is in the autumn when apples are plentiful and cheap. Peel and core the apples. Slice them making the slices reasonably thick. Fit them into the oven on kebab skewers. Make sure they are not touching each other and that the warm air is circulating all around them. Turn the oven down very low. The apple rings are ready when they are completely dry on the outside. It takes about five hours to dry apple rings. The longer and more slowly they are dried the better. The edges may become slightly brown. Don't put them into the fridge or freezer: store them in an airtight container in a cool, dry place.

APPLE CAKE

5 oz. (1¼ cup) wholewheat flour
4 oz. (½ cup) butter or margarine
2 eggs
about 5 oz. (1 cup) apple rings
4 oz. (½ cup) brown sugar
1 tsp. baking powder
water

Cream the fat and sugar until white and fluffy. Gradually beat in the eggs. Mix in the flour and baking powder. Add a little water to soften the mixture. Cut the apple rings in half and arrange them in overlapping rows on the bottom of a greased Swiss roll tin. Sprinkle with a little cinnamon and sugar. Pour the mixture into the tin on top of arranged rings. Bake in a moderate oven, 375°F or gas mark 5, for 30 minutes.

CANDIED PEEL

Use the leftover rinds of limes, lemons or oranges. Soak the rinds of four oranges in slightly salt water for three days.

Drain, rinse and boil until tender (about 10 mins.). Boil two large cups of sugar and one of water for 5 minutes. Place the rinds in a basin, cover with the syrup. Leave to stand for two days. Strain off and boil the syrup. Add the rinds until they become semi-transparent—it will take about fifteen minutes.

Place the rinds on a dish. Pour some of the syrup into each skin. Sprinkle them with caster (extra-fine) sugar and dry them off in a slightly warm oven.

Store in an airtight container.

FROSTED FRUITS

These are difficult to store. They should be made and eaten within the same period as fresh fruit. Use small fruits such as grapes or slices of orange and grapefruit in bunches or as individual pieces.

Wash the fruit. Stir an egg white but don't beat it. Brush the fruit all over with the egg white. Cover with caster (extra-fine) sugar and allow to dry. Arrange on a dish.

SUGAR PLUMS

These are plums preserved in the autumn by soaking and draining them several times in a rich syrup. Prunes can be reconstituted to make sugar plums.

Take a pound of the largest prunes, a pound of sugar and the juice of half a lemon. Stone the prunes, keeping them whole, and steam them for

3 eggs
3 oz. ($\frac{1}{3}$ cup) caster (fine) sugar
2 oz. ($\frac{1}{2}$ cup) self-raising flour

2 tsp. cocoa
pinch of salt

Heat the oven. Grease and line a Swiss roll tin. Whisk eggs and sugar until thick and fluffy. Sift in the flour and then gently stir in the cocoa. Spread the mixture evenly over the tin. Bake for 10 minutes at 400°F or gas mark 6.

Cool slightly and turn out on to greaseproof paper. Trim the ends and roll it carefully but firmly with the sheet of greaseproof paper. If the Swiss roll breaks, don't panic. It can be mended later with the icing. Leave it to cool.

THE ICING

Melt 4 oz. (1 cup) of cocoa in two tablespoons of water over a low heat. Leave it to cool. Beat in $\frac{1}{2}$ lb. (1 cup) of butter or soft margarine. Beat in $\frac{1}{2}$ lb. (1$\frac{3}{4}$ cup) of icing (confectioner's) sugar.

Unroll the sponge. Spread some of the mixture over and re-roll. Coat the Swiss roll with the rest of the mixture. Pattern the 'bark' by using a fork. Sift a little icing sugar on to the log to represent snow.

about 40 minutes, or until plump. Cover in a bowl with boiling water. Stand for 10 minutes, then put back to steam until plump again.

Sprinkle some icing (confectioner's) sugar on a dish. Spear a prune with a fork, and coat with icing sugar. Allow syrup to drip back into saucepan. Dip the prunes again. Cool overnight and wrap in seal-wrap.

Individually wrapped sugar plums make charming baubles for the tree. One or two can be used as stocking fillers.

THE YULE LOG

The tradition of bringing a huge log into the house made good sense. It was as important to the old housewife to get a good fire started for spit roasting the meat just as the modern housewife needs a reliable oven. The log was taken from any local wood available. Once it was dragged indoors the men could relax and enjoy their ale, while the women busied themselves preparing the Christmas feast.

A miniature Yule log makes a charming decoration as a centrepiece for the table. Find a small log—it doesn't need to be evenly shaped. Chop or sand the base of the log to make it stand flat. Stand it on a firm piece of card. Drill three holes in the top to make candle holders. Glue on sprigs of holly, mistletoe and ivy. Add a few fir cones to the sides. Paint it with shoe whitener to make snow.

You can also make a Yule log from a Swiss roll as a festive treat. The quickest way to make one is by buying a ready-made Swiss roll and covering it with some chocolate butter icing. But chocolate logs are fun and easy to make, and it will keep children busy if they help make one.

DRINKS

Alcoholic beverages have been associated with the festivities around Christmas for centuries. Even Father Christmas was first pictured with a glass or two.

FROSTY GLASSES

If everyone is offered the same drink such as champagne cocktail (a little brandy and a lot of champagne), prepare some festive glasses. Take two basins. Put some water in one, and some sugar in the other. Dip the rim of the glass first in the water and then in the sugar. Chill the glasses and set ready on a tray.

PUNCH

The punch bowl began to take the place of the wassail bowl in the seventeenth century. The wassail bowl was a large communal drinking bowl. Punch bowls were designed with the glasses hanging from the sides. Their ladles often had a coin inserted, a symbol of the coins which were offered with the wassail. It was more likely that a spiced ale formed the basis of the wassail instead of wine as in a modern punch recipe.

In making punch, the juice of several lemons, together with one lemon cut into slices, is put with sugar into boiling water, allowed to stand for half an hour then strained into the bowl, and the spirits added, rum, brandy, gin, or whisky with some grated nutmeg. The recipes vary, the quantities of each ingredient required being more or less a matter of taste; the proportion of water to spirits may be two to one, or less. Rum and brandy may be mixed, sometimes milk takes the place of water, or champagne is used instead of spirits. Egg punch is made by adding four eggs to each pint of whisky, brandy and rum in equal proportions.

Sally's Simple Punch Mix in a clean pail in the kitchen. Serve in a Victorian wash bowl. Mix together three bottles of white wine, three bottles of lemonade and half a bottle of vodka. Float lemon, mint leaves, cucumber and slices of apple on the top. Serve chilled.

From The Ladies' Treasury 1880

Punch.
The old recipe to make punch is a very reliable one, only add to it so much sweetened claret that will make it of a pretty rose colour, or deep ruby, in preference—
One of sour,
Two of sweet,
Four of strong,
Eight of weak.
Use a wine glass, a teacup or other measure, for all the ingredients. Say a large wine glass full of strained lemon juice, two of broken loaf sugar, two of brandy, and two of gin, and eight of the same measure of cold boiled water. The sugar must first be dissolved in the water, then the whole be mixed together, adding the spirit last. The sweetened claret is added after the punch is made. The mixture may now take the name of 'Rosalio'. In the proportion given, it is impossible (with claret added) to say what the drink is, for it resembles nothing but itself—only it is very seductive, not one flavour predominating above another.'

EGGNOG

This warming drink was often served to invalids and forms a meal in itself. Beat up an egg. Strain it into a tumbler and add two teaspoonsful of brandy and one teaspoonful of caster (fine) sugar. Top up the tumbler with half a pint of scalded milk.

The following is a recipe for cold eggnog.

4 oz. (½ cup) sugar	¼ pint (½ cup) golden rum or
3 eggs	tbsp. rum or brandy
¼ tsp. salt	flavouring
ground nutmeg	16 fl. oz. (2 cups) light cream

Beat egg yolks, adding sugar and salt gradually, until the mixture is thick and creamy. Stir in cream and rum, and chill at least 3 hours. Just before serving, sprinkle with nutmeg.

MULLED WINE

Heating, sweetening and seasoning wine or other liquor with spices is called mulling. In the days of hearth fires, mulling used to be done by plunging a red hot poker from the coals into the wine.

Nowadays, the wine is heated very gently, without bringing it to the boil, and by adding a pinch of nutmeg, and other spices if desired, and a pinch of sugar.

A SNOWBALL

Pour a little Advocaat into a tumbler. Fill with fizzy lemonade (7-Up), leaving enough room at the top for the foam.

PART V
THE FESTIVITIES

Make we merry, both more and less,   Some other sport then let him bring.
For now is the time of Christmas!   That it may please at this feasting.
If that he say he cannot sing,   For now is the time of Christmas!

A·HAPPY·CHRISTMAS·

FAR BEST OF ALL THE CHRISTMAS FUN

THE MERRY DANCE WHEN DINNER'S DONE

GAMES

Games can be played at any time during the festivities, though they are usually reserved for after Christmas dinner. Try some of the following games which are easy to organize and can be played by a small family as well as a great crowd.

RAFFLES

These were popular in Victorian households. Give everyone a numbered ticket and put an identical number into a hat. Some families fix the winners so that all the children win a numbered prize from the tree. It can be great fun to fix the winners so that grumpy old uncle wins the fairy from the top of the tree and a child who resists washing wins a miniature bar of soap labelled 'a year's supply of soap'.

FORFEITS

Collect an item from every player such as a shoe, a bracelet or a tie. Each player must win back their possessions by performing a forfeit.

Hold up the first item and say: 'I have a thing, a very pretty thing, the owner of this pretty thing must crawl around the room crying like a baby; stand on his head and sing the National Anthem; pat his head and rub his tummy at the same time; or (most hated by children who detest kisses) kiss everyone under the mistletoe.' Children enjoy helping to make a list of forfeits before the game begins.

CHARADES

This game was played at Christmas time in every Victorian family. Youngsters went to endless trouble to select a difficult word and to prepare the sketches and the costumes.

The family divides into two teams. Each team selects a double-syllable word. Each team acts out three short sketches. The first sketch portrays the first syllable of the word, the second sketch the second syllable, and the third sketch the whole word. The opposing team must then guess the word chosen by the acting team.

Charades are fun to play in a large family or group but difficult to organize in a small one. Try the modern version of this game for a small family. Each player takes a turn at miming the title of a play, a book or a film. Each word of the title must be mimed until it has been guessed by the other players. The winner is the person who guesses the whole title.

BLIND MAN'S BUFF

There are reports of this game being played during the Twelve Days of Christmas as long ago as the middle of the sixteenth century. Like all the best games it's very easy to prepare. Find a scarf for the blindfold. Choose a player to be the blind man. Spin him round three times. He then wanders the room blindly trying to catch someone. When the blind man does catch someone he must guess who it is. If he's correct, that player then becomes the blind man. If he's wrong he must go on to catch someone else.

SQUEAK, PIGGY, SQUEAK!

This game is an ancient one and played in a similar way to Blind Man's Buff. Players sit in a circle on chairs. A player is blindfolded. He takes a cushion and places it on someone's lap and sits down on it. Without touching the victim—as it may be easy to guess who it is—the blindfolded player demands, 'Squeak, piggy, squeak!' He must guess from the squeak whose lap he is sitting on. Little children adore this game, especially when an adult sits down on them!

WHO'S UNDER THE BLANKET?

This is an easy party game to organize. Send one player out of the room, and hide a player under the blanket. (You can disguise a very small person with some cushions.) The player must guess who's under the blanket without touching them. It helps to cause confusion by hiding two or three other persons behind the sofa.

SKITTLES

Rinse some beer or coke cans to use as the skittles and drain them well. Make a ball from a sheet of rolled-up newspaper. Stand the skittles in a row along one wall. Place a Christmas streamer down

on the floor as a marker. Players stand behind the streamer, and a score is made if a beer can is knocked down. A player is out when they fail to hit anything. The winner gets a cracker. The eldest member of the family should keep the score and allow no second chances. He can allow a second or third game.

FLOUR PUDDING

Little children hate this game and older children love it. Fill a pudding basin with flour, and then place a plate on the top and tip the pudding on to the plate. Place one square of chocolate on the top of the pudding. Spread plenty of newspaper on the kitchen floor and place the pudding on it. The players sit in a ring around the pudding, and each player in turn takes the knife and slices a little out of the pudding. The player who makes the piece of chocolate collapse into the pudding wins it—*but*, he must pick it up with his teeth!

TREASURE HUNT

One game which children can organize when they can read and write is a treasure hunt around the house. Match the non-reader with an adult or the game will be unfair. The organizers must judge and supervise a treasure hunt and not compete. The most important job for the organizer is to ensure that every player puts the clues back exactly where they found them, or the next player is cheated. The clues can be very simple. 'Go to the place where we put the rubbish', or 'Knock on the "ring, ring, ring"'

HUNT THE SLIPPER AND HUNT THE THIMBLE

The Victorians were very fond of these games. Everyone could join in, and it wasn't always the clever and witty who won. One player stays in the room and hides a slipper, thimble—or a fir cone would be suitable. Everyone else searches. The winner is the one who finds the object first and then it's their turn to hide it.

THE FIRST BALLOON

Many cottagers kept a pig which routed for scraps in the garden. When it was killed for the table, no part of it was wasted. Every edible piece of meat was eaten—from the offal to the trotters. The skin was cured to make purses and pouches (which is why pigskin purses and wallets make appropriate gifts still). The first balloons were made from the pig's

bladder. The pig's bladder balloon made a toy for humble children and joke material for court jesters. A favourite joke was to fill the balloon with water and leave it on the floor, anticipating that someone wouldn't be able to resist giving the balloon a kick, causing an explosion of water and very wet feet.

Games with balloons offer some really traditional fun. You can pass a balloon from person to person, under the chin without using your hands. You can run with a balloon between your knees as a forfeit, or sit on a balloon to burst it.

which can be either the front door or the telephone. Ten clues to find around the house are quite enough to make a good game and ensure that none of the adults drop out from exhaustion.

At Christmas time of course the final clue leads to Christmas treasure, which can be one mince pie or a cracker.

TRICKS

When someone takes off their thumb or shows around a thumb in a matchbox, we know the Lord of Misrule is busy.

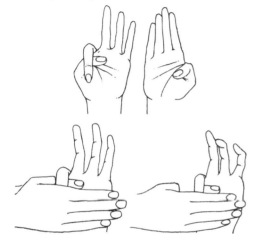

To remove your thumb, hold the left hand out, palm upwards, with the fingers together. Bend the top joint of the thumb down into the palm and fit the second joint of the right-hand thumb to it, covering the gap with the index finger of the right hand. Separate the two thumbs by moving your right hand away and then replace it against the left thumb.

Thumb in a matchbox Make a large hole in both base sections of a matchbox. Line well with cotton wool, leaving a hole to poke your thumb through. Ask if anyone would like to see it, and slide the drawer open.

CARD TRICKS

Reversing a card This is a simple card trick, requiring no sleight of hand. Place a king, queen and knave face up on a table. Tell your audience

tell your audience, are four inns. These are placed in a row on the table. The four kings each visits an inn—and you place a king on top of each ace. As the kings must have a royal escort, a knave accompanies each—and again you place a knave on top of each king. But alas! The four queens are suspicious of their husbands' intentions and they follow the rest to the inns. You now have four piles on the table, each containing an ace, a king, a knave, and a queen. These piles are picked up and placed in your left hand, one after the other. Apparently there was a quarrel at each of the inns until each of the respective parties were separated—and you ask someone from the audience to cut the pack in any place he wishes, replacing the two halves immediately. Then deal out the cards once more into four piles. To the amazement of your audience they will quite naturally turn up in piles of four aces, four kings, four knaves, and four queens. The pack may be cut as often as your audience may wish, but the cards will nevertheless turn up in this order.

PLAY-ACTING

One of the things children love doing is dressing up and acting out a short play or skit, and this can easily be planned for an afternoon's entertainment for the rest of the family. Children can use discarded clothing as costumes, or you can try some of the following ideas for making costumes and 'props'.

one of the cards. On your return you will be able to tell them which of the cards was reversed. The method by which you can detect the move is elementary. Examine the court cards in a pack and you will notice that the white margin of each is slightly narrower on one side than the other. If you place the cards so that all the narrow sides are on a corresponding position, it will then be easy to tell which of the cards has been reversed.

Naughty knaves Sort out the four knaves. Fan them out to show the audience, hiding three more random cards behind them. Place the rest of the pack face down on the table. Tell a simple story about the naughty knaves. Place the seven cards face down at the top of the pack. The first knave (one of the three random cards) goes to rob the ground floor of the pack. The second knave (one of the three random ones) goes to rob the ground floor of the pack, and the third knave (the third random card) goes to rob the top floor. The last knave stays on the roof as lookout. Turn up the last

that you will leave the room and ask them to reverse (first) knave to show the audience. The police are coming. The first knave calls the others. Tap the top of the pack. Turn over the four knaves which mysteriously appear all together on top of the pack.

Identifying the court cards This trick is simple enough for a child to master and have fun impressing the adults. Ask some member of the audience to blindfold you and then sit at a table with a conspirator next to you. Tell someone to shuffle the cards and then deal them out face upwards on to the table. Look up at the ceiling and tell the audience that, although you cannot see the pack, you will indicate when a court card is thrown on the table. Each time a court card appears, your secret companion gives you a kick under the table, and you can then indicate accordingly. If done with showmanship, this trick can be remarkably effective.

A royal trip Take from a pack of cards all four aces, kings, queens and knaves. The four aces, you

Plaits are easy to make from wool. Make thick plaits for a princess or one dark plait and a trailing moustache, for a mandarin. Make a wild wool wig for a shipwrecked sailor or a bright orange wig for a clown.

Masks need to fit perfectly or children won't be able to see out of the eye holes. The basic materials required are simply shirring elastic and card. Make a plain black mask for a highwayman or robber and a sequin-studded mask, edged with lace, for a beautiful lady. Make a single black eyepatch for a pirate. Add two curtain rings for earrings with shirring elastic to go over the ears. Make animal masks for very young children. A timid child loves to be a fierce lion once in a while.

Cloaks of every kind can be made from old silk, velvet or brocade curtains. They will suit kings, queens, princes, princesses, magicians, witches knights, ladies or wandering beggars.

Any child who plays 'Hospital' will be thrilled with a roll of bandage, a sling or a few wooden tongue depressers and a disposable hypodermic syringe.

FAMILY TREE

It has always been the tradition for old people to tell stories to the young people and children in the family at Christmas time. Although we can't all spend twelve years researching our roots as Alex Haley did, we can tell the young people as much as we can remember about our immediate ancestors. It can become a fascinating game working out the family tree. We all like to know about our origins: it makes us feel secure. Old people have excellent memories for the distant past.

Family heirlooms, when the elderly finally feel they should pass them on into safe hands, must be the most wonderful Christmas gifts which can be given or received. It makes a tangible link with the past and gives enormous pleasure to both giver and receiver.

BOXING DAY

Traditionally Boxing Day has become an important day for all winter sporting activities from football matches to hunting. Legend has it that the first game of football was played in Kingston-upon-Thames. A band of Vikings made their way up the Thames pillaging and looting, but the citizens of Kingston were ready for them. A bloody battle ensued and the Vikings were defeated. The townsfolk decapitated the Viking chief, and the young men of the town triumphantly kicked the head from one end of the town to the other. The following year the same young men commemorated their victory with a free-for-all game using a leather ball. It became an annual event.

All kinds of football games and novelties are offered to small boys as gifts at Christmas time. One of the best games which the whole family can play is still a game of blow football.

TWELVE DAYS OF CHRISTMAS

From Christmas until Epiphany, 6th January, it was the custom to feast and entertain and to be entertained. Punch and Judy shows abounded, the pantomime was introduced by the Victorians, and fancy dress parties and balls were held.

The song, 'The Twelve Days of Christmas' was first published in England in about 1780 in *Mirth Without Mischief*. So its history is not as ancient as we sometimes suppose. It's described as a memory and forfeit game.

The leader of the game commenced by saying the lines of 'The First Day', and they were repeated by each member of the company in turn, then the leader said the second and the first days together, which were similarly repeated round the circle. This was continued until the lines for the twelve days were said by every player. For each mistake a forfeit was demanded in the manner of 'The play of the wide-mouth waddling frog'.

On the first day of Christmas, my true love sent to me,
A partridge in a pear tree.
On the second day of Christmas, my true love sent to me,
Two turtle doves and a partridge in a pear tree.

Three French hens,
Four colley birds,

Five gold rings,
Six geese a-laying,
Seven swans a-swimming,
Eight maids a-milking,
Nine drummers drumming,
Ten pipers piping,
Eleven ladies dancing,
Twelve lords a-leaping.

There are many colloquial versions of this song in France which suggests that it probably came across the Channel from the French court.

When playing 'The Twelve Days' as a family forfeit game, remember that very young children find it extremely difficult to memorize the reverse order of the words. Let them play the part of the Lord of Misrule and select forfeits for other members of the family.

BOXING DAY

St Stephen was sentenced to be stoned to death around AD 36 for his Christian faith and became the first Christian martyr. His saint's day is now commemorated by the Church on the day after Christmas.

Poor Boxes were kept in every church. On Boxing Day the poor gathered at the church door to receive their Boxing Day gifts. The old, the poor and lame relied upon their gifts from the church Poor Box to help them through the winter months. It was also a day when wealthy people would gather their servants together in the morning to present them with their Christmas Boxes, usually in the form of money. Hence the title of 'Boxing Day'.

THE CIRCUS

Many families make a traditional visit to the circus at Christmas time. The circus is a direct descendant of the Roman games, and the animals, trapeze artists and fire-eaters give the clue to this. Since Roman occupation the British have been going to the circus—little wonder that it has become a firmly established tradition. In the old-time circus lives were thrown away to entertain the audience. Many of the early Christians were thrown to the lions in the Roman circus. There is more than a glimpse of death-defying daring in most circus acts.

THE PANTOMIME

It used to be the custom for families to make an outing to the theatre to see a pantomime on Boxing Day. The pantomime is a living lesson in the history of the English theatre. The word *mime* gives the clue to the origins. Miming (or mumming) was performed by travelling bands of mummers. They took over the early theatre when priests banished biblical plays from the church and churchyard. It was St Paul who decreed that women should never preach in a place of worship. By the time the mummers took over the early plays the custom of young men playing the roles of women in the stories had become firmly established. Obviously if a man play-acted in church it was a form of preaching. When Shakespeare's plays were first performed young men always took the female roles—we still see this today when a pantomime dame is played by a man.

The pantomime horse or cow, played by two actors, is a relic from the old hobby horse which frolicked in May Day celebrations playing jokes on the audience. Today the role of the hero is played by a girl. This custom is less than two hundred years old. It made good commercial sense to have a glamorous hero, with a fine contralto voice and good legs.

When plays were performed on the village green

tumblers, jugglers and performing bears would have been working independently to catch the attention of the audience watching the play. Today no one is surprised when the story of the pantomime suddenly stops and on come the high-wire artists or the daring young man on the flying trapeze. The early mummers wisely integrated the other performers into their own play.

In the best tradition there is always plenty of audience participation. The players throw things at the audience and they throw them back; the players make asides to the audience as if they're the only people who know what's happening on the stage. 'He's behind you' scream the children at the tops of their voices to warn the hero against the villain of the piece. Good triumphs over Evil and everyone lives happily ever after.

AND A HAPPY NEW YEAR

The ancient Romans set the date for the western world to celebrate the new year. The first day of January was given over to the worship of the two-faced god, Janus. He looked backwards at the old year passing and forward to the new year coming. Janus is now represented by Old Father Tyme who arrives at midnight accompanied by the bright, fresh, cherubic 'New Year'—full of promise.

Scotland was never subjected to Roman occupation. It was the Romans who expressed some of the worst excesses during the long dark nights of Saturnalia and English winters. The Scottish Calvinistic influence of the sixteenth century encouraged a puritanical attitude towards Christmas festivities. Consequently Christmas passes quietly in Scotland to this day. In place of Christmas festivities Scotsmen, all over the world, have become the masters of ceremonies in celebrating the New Year.

HOGMANAY

In Scotland on New Year's Eve it's traditionally open house in every home. In the evening the table is laid with choice food and the glasses are ready to welcome whoever comes to drink a New Year toast. Many toasts with malt whisky are made to the New Year and many taken. The celebrations go on well into the early hours of New Year's Day.

The 'first footer' The first man across the threshold after midnight on New Year's Eve brings a lump of coal and good luck. Long ago the first footer brought a lump of salt as well. It was essential to the well-being of the family that they had plenty of both these commodities for the coming year.

A tall dark-haired man was in popular demand as a first footer. It would have been bad luck to open the door to a blond helmeted Viking who had come to steal the cattle and the farm. The taller and darker the first footer the greater the luck he brings.

From Robert Chambers in *Popular Rhymes of Scotland* (published in 1869) we learn: 'Busy housewives prepared an excess of honest fare in preparation for Hogmanay. It was no unpleasing scene, during the forenoon, to see children going home laden, each with his large apron bellying out before him stuffed full of cakes, and perhaps scarcely able to waddle under the load.'

And of course there is always a rhyme or a chant in the best tradition of children when they have something special to celebrate. The modern child chants:

A happy new year, a bottle of beer,
A slap on the ear that will do 'til next year.

If this sounds slightly unfriendly try the rhyme which can be traced back to the time of Mary Queen of Scots:

Rise up auld wives, and shake yer feathers,
Dinna think that we are beggars,
We're just wee bairns come out to play,
Rise up and gi'e's oor Hogmanay.

Collecting the bellying apron of goodies is typical of children. Too young to stay up to enjoy all the sweetmeats of First Footing they go around the following afternoon gathering up the leftovers.

ALMOND SHORTBREAD

Shortbread is a traditional Scottish dish which is simple to make and very tasty.

5 oz. (¾ cup) butter	8 oz. (2 cups) plain
1 oz. (¼ cup) ground	flour
almonds	1 oz. (¼ cup) cornflour
3 oz. (⅓ cup) sugar	(cornstarch)

Cream the fat in a bowl, add the almonds. Sift the flour and the cornflour. Gradually work them into the creamed fat with the sugar, using the hand. Knead on a board, and roll out ¼ in. thick. Cut into rounds or fancy shapes. Allow to firm for about 1 hour. Bake in a moderate oven, 350°F or gas mark 4 for 20 to 30 minutes.

The finished shortbread should be golden brown. Allow the shortbread to cool before turning it out, but mark the sections for breaking while it's hot. Store in an airtight tin.

When serving, pile up the pieces and top with a tartan ribbon as a centrepiece for the table on New Year's Eve.

TWELFTH-NIGHT

This was the last night of the Christmas festivities. The revelry and feasting reached a climax on Twelfth-night, which is traditionally the date given for the arrival of the wise men to the manger, bringing their gifts of gold, myrrh and frankincense.

The gold was the symbol of the man born to be king. Myrrh, the bitter herb, was the symbol of the bitterness of the crucifixion, and the frankincense symbolized the holy man.

The feast of Epiphany was traditionally the night for dancing, singing and family parties Today we have a tradition that all decorations must be taken down by Twelfth-night or the family will have bad luck for the coming year.

The Twelfth-night cake has become the Christmas cake. There are no references to any Christmas cakes in history. Mrs Beeton was still baking a Twelfth-night cake. It was the highlight of the Twelfth-night feast. Into it were stirred tiny silver charms, a pea and a bean which were fortune tellers.

The young lady who found the wedding bells inside her slice of cake would be hearing wedding bells in the coming year. The anchor symbolized a journey, the bachelor's button was for a bachelor and the thimble was for an old maid. Whoever found the pea and the bean led the dancing. This was based on the tradition of appointing a Lord of Misrule.

A Twelfth-night party would have been something to look forward to when the feasting and present-giving was over.

MRS BEETON'S TWELFTH-NIGHT CAKE

6 oz. (¾ cup) butter or	4 oz. (¾ cup) of currants
margarine	mixed peel
3 oz. (⅓ cup) brown sugar	sultanas
3 eggs	½ level tsp. each of
½ gill milk	mixed spice and
1 level tsp. bicarbonate	ground cinnamon
of soda	¾ lb. (3 cups) plain flour
2 oz. (⅛ cup) treacle	¼ tsp. salt

Line a 7″ cake tin with greaseproof paper. Cream the fat and sugar until soft and white. Gently beat in the eggs. Dissolve the soda in the milk. Add the milk and the treacle and beat thoroughly. Add the fruit and spices. Lightly stir in the flour and salt. Bake in a warm oven, 335°F or gas mark 3. Bake silver charms in the cake. Cooking time two to two and a half hours.

CLEARING UP

When good King Arthur ruled this land,
He was a goodly king;
He stole three pecks of barley meal
To make a bag pudding.

A bag pudding the king did make,
And stuffed it well with plums;
And in it put great lumps of fat,
As big as my two thumbs.

The king and queen did eat thereof, ·
And noblemen beside;
And what they could not eat that night,
The queen next morning fried.

Leftovers of Christmas pudding 1. Stand the cold Christmas pudding in a little milk. Leave it until the milk is absorbed. Cover it with foil and heat through in a warm oven. 2. Cut the pudding into slices. Heat a little butter in a frying pan. Fry gently on both sides until it is heated through.

Rissoles Mince 6 oz. of cold turkey meat, add two shallots or a small onion. Add three sprigs of parsley. Make a thick sauce with 1 oz. of butter, 1½ tablespoons of stock, 1 tablespoon lemon juice and seasoning of salt and pepper. A pinch of ground mace will add to the flavour.

Add the minced meat to the stock sauce, mix and spread on a plate to cool.

Roll a dessertspoonful of the mixture into a sausage shape. Roll in egg and breadcrumbs. Fry until golden on all sides.

Bubble-and-squeak In the olden days, when Monday was traditionally wash day, bubble-and-squeak was always served for dinner with slices of cold meat from the Sunday joint. It makes an ideal dish to serve with cold slices of turkey on Boxing Day.

Save all the leftover vegetables from the Christmas dinner. Heat a little butter in a frying pan. Toss leftover peas, Brussels sprouts, creamed potatoes and roast potatoes into the hot fat. Cook over a medium heat until the mixture is nicely browned. In our house we call this 'Poor Man's Ratatouille'.

Leftover fruit Citrus fruit stays fresh if it is kept somewhere cool. It can be used up slowly in general cooking.

Soft fruit such as grapes, pears, apples and bananas soon rot if they are left in a fruit bowl in a warm room. Fruit salad is a popular dessert to serve on Boxing Day, using fruit which decorated the table the day before.

Finely peel a lemon. Cut it in half. Cover it in a saucepan with water and a level tablespoon of sugar. Simmer for about 20 minutes. Strain off the lemon. Use the liquid as a base for the fruit salad. Peel all the fruit, removing pips and inner skins. Cut grapes in half and remove pips. This fruit salad can be kept in an air-tight container in the fridge for some time as the lemon syrup prevents discoloration. Add sliced bananas at the last moment or they turn black. Serve with leftover brandy sauce, fresh cream or custard (or all three for a lavish feast).

Pine-needle essence It's a shame to burn the Christmas tree if it can't be planted out in the garden. Get the last little bit of essence out of the pine needles.

Let children strip off handfuls of pines. Crush them with a pestle and mortar or with a wooden spoon in a bowl.

Put the needles into a screw-top glass jar and cover them with corn oil. Add a teaspoonful of vodka. Stand the jar in warm washing-up water every day for a week. Give the mixture a good shake from time to time. Strain off the needles. The oil remaining will have a lovely tangy pine smell. Use it as a bath oil or shake a little into some hand cream. (If the oil is really pungent bottle some and save it for candle-making next year. A few drops added to candles will fill the house with the spicy aroma of pine.)

A pine-needle pattern Collect a handful of fallen pine needles. Paste a small section of a sheet of paper. Press on the pine-needle pattern. Keep pasting and pattern-making until the page is covered.

A Christmas tree with roots Water the tree now and again whilst it is indoors to prevent it drying out too much. It will be important to carry out a planting ceremony in the garden. Make it a right royal occasion. The family may not have a golden spade but there will certainly be several helpers who will be honoured to dig a little. Give the tree a good drink. Stamp the soil well down around the roots to stop the moisture from evaporating too quickly. In a dry spring the Christmas tree will need watering.

Old Christmas cards Whatever else is thrown away during the massive clear up don't throw away any Christmas cards. Naturally some households have no further use for them. If yours is one of these, bundle up the cards and take them into the local playgroup, nursery or primary school when you're passing. The children will find lots of ways to recycle them.

Crawling babies and toddlers need a watchful eye kept on them at Christmas time. Take special care over scissors, plastic, wire, glitter and other bright materials. Non-toxic paint, smooth edges on wood and no tiny pieces are important points to notice. Ensure that an open fire has a safe guard and that candles are kept out of children's reach. Tree decorations are also irresistible to children, and it would be wise to choose only non-breakable decorations.

For permission to reproduce illustrations we are grateful to the following:

Barnaby's Picture Library; The British Library; Camera Press; Courtauld Institute of Art; Fortnum & Mason Ltd; Hirschsprung Collection, Copenhagen; J. Sainsbury Ltd; Keystone Press Agency; Mansell Collection; National Library of Scotland; Novosti; Pollock's Toy Museum; Popperfoto; Radio Times Hulton Picture Library; Raphael Tuck and Sons Ltd, Blackpool; Tom Smith & Co. Ltd; Victoria and Albert Museum.

Illustrations by Jonathan Wolstenholme:
pp. 13, 14(r), 15(r), 16, 17, 21(l + c), 22(c + r), 25(l), 28–9, 30, 31(r), 34, 38(bot. r), 39, 40, 41, 42, 43, 44, 45, 46, 50(r), 55, 56, 57, 58(r), 59(r), 60, 61(l), 62, 63, 64, 65, 66(c + r), 67(r), 70, 82(r), 89(l), 92(r),

Designed by Bernard Higton

Music arranged by Eira Davies